LAST SHIP TO PROXIMA CENTAURI

Greg Lam

BROADWAY PLAY PUBLISHING INC
New York
www.broadwayplaypublishing.com
info@broadwayplaypublishing.com

Cover art: Kitchen Dog Theater

First edition: May 2023
I S B N: 978-0-88145-982-1

Book design: Marie Donovan
Page make-up: Adobe InDesign
Typefaces: Palatino & YaHei

In loving memory of
The United States of America

Special thanks to the translators: Livian Yeh, Jecenia
Isis Figueroa, and Kayodé Soyemi.

LAST SHIP TO PROXIMA CENTAURI received
its world digital premiere at Kitchen Dog Theater
(Christopher Carlos & Tina Parker, Artistic Directors;
Tim Johnson, Managing Director) in Dallas running
from 25 February-4 March 2021. The cast and creative
contributors were:

EMERSON ....Max Hartman
RUSSELL .... Tina Parker
HENRY .... Mark Quach
TUNDE/CONTROL..Lee George
PAZ/CONTROL .... Liza Marie Gonzalez

Director .... Tina Parker
Stage Manager/Tech Director..................... Jeremy Escobar
Set design ....Jocelyn Girigorie
Lighting design .... Aaron Johansen
Costume design ....Melissa Panzarello
Composers/Sound design .... Ancient Futures
Prop design .... Cindy Ernst Godinez
Choreography....................................... Danielle Georgiou
Mandarin Coaches .... Heidi Shen & Mike Wang
Film production .... Jonathan Taylor
& team from Karve Media

LAST SHIP TO PROXIMA CENTAURI received its theatrical world premiere production at Portland Stage Company (Anita Stewart, Executive & Artistic Director) in Maine running from 2-20 March 2022. The cast and creative contributors were:

EMERSON .... Tom Ford
RUSSELL ....Marcy McGuigan
HENRY ....Kennedy Kanagawa
TUNDE/CONTROL.. Jamal James
PAZ/CONTROL .... Octavia Chavez-Richmond

Director ....Kevin R Free
Stage Manager .... Myles C Hatch
Set design .... German Cardenas-Alaminos
Lighting design ....Jamie Grant
Sound design...Seth Asa Sengel
Costume design .... Haydee Zelideth
Intimacy Coordinator ....Hannah Cordes
Casting Director .... Jenn Haltman
Fight Choreographer .... Sally Wood
Projection Designer .... Mike Post
Mandarin Coach ....Mao Ding

CHARACTERS

MORRIS EMERSON, *50, the pilot of the ship, white American man. Gregarious. Pretty good at his job. Loves America, dammit. Speaks English only.*

ADELAIDE "ADDIE" RUSSELL, *55, the Captain of the ship, Emerson's superior, white American woman. Calm and calculating. Wears her responsibility well. Speaks English and Spanish she learned in high school long ago (imperfectly at best).*

CONTROL 1, *a stern voice of the control room on Proxima Centuari. Speaks English well but with perhaps an accent as it is a second language.*

CONTROL 2, *a more friendly voice of the control room on Proxima Centuari. Speaks English well but with perhaps an accent as it is a second language.*

HENRY HIRANO, *25, a graduate student of law. Japanese-American man. He gets along with most anyone, or at least he tries to. Speaks English only.*

TUNDE, *[toon-day], 30-45, a security officer. Native of Proxima Centauri. Enthusiastic admirer of American culture but does not let that cloud his judgement. Mixed race, but prominently African. Male. The name is Yoruba Nigerian in origin, short for Obotunde ("Son has returned"). Speaks multiple languages, including perfect Mandarin and Yoruba, adequate but stilted English, and a smattering of Spanish.*

PAZ, 30-45, *another security officer. Native of Proxima Centauri. Fearful of newcomers, specifically whites and males, and feels no compunction to moderate her feelings toward them. Mixed race, but prominently Latinx. Female. Impatient. Always on guard. The name is Spanish for "Peace". Speaks Mandarin and Spanish flawlessly.*

PAZ *and* TUNDE *occasionally drop in phrases from different languages they know, usually for exclamations or when searching for words.* PAZ, *Spanish and Chinese;* TUNDE *Chinese, English, and Yoruba.*

RECORDED VOICES: *the computer virtual assistant's voice (LANA), welcome beacon in several languages, passenger wakeup sequence,* "MORGAN FREEMAN"

Cast Doubling: It's assumed that roles will be doubled as follows: one actor plays the roles of PAZ *and one of the* CONTROL *voices. Another actor plays the roles of* TUNDE *and the other* CONTROL *voice. The recorded voices can be recorded in advance. Currently* CONTROL 2 *has the Indian female name of "Manisha", but it can be changed to suit the actor's gender and background as necessary. For example: "Manish", the male version of the name, is one possibility. The derisive nicknames could then be "Mannish" and "Mashuna Matata" or "Manischewitz".*

Note: I do not denote the exact place where actors could/ should interrupt other actors' lines during tense, overlapping arguments. Other playwrights sometimes denote this with a slash in a line that is interruptable. But there are certainly plenty of places where interruptions can happen, and you have my broad permission to deploy interruptions.

SETTING

*ACT ONE the set is the bridge of a spaceship. The first thing
you notice about the control room is that it is unbelievably
cramped. There is barely enough room to move around. The
second thing is that it is very worn, having been in continual
use for literally 2000 years by roughly 100 pilots. Things
have been damaged, jury rigged and repaired and duct taped.*

It's not the sleek and spacious **Star Trek** *bridge. It's closer to
the cockpit of a modern day airplane with real controls and
steering mechanisms. There is one exit to the rear.*

*In addition to the seating and controls in front, there's a
communication station and an entertainment station in
the back with a large screen. If language indications or
translations are used, it can be on this screen. Windows to
the outside reveal a view of deep space.*

*ACT TWO the set is the same bridge of the spaceship after
the ship has crashed. (/spoilers) Everything is damaged and
askew. A large window has busted open, revealing blue
sky and daylight. The many lights that indicated computer
activity are out.*

NOTES ABOUT TRANSLATED TEXT

This script includes dialogue that has been translated into Chinese (by playwright Livian Yeh), Spanish (by playwright Jecenia Isis Figueroa), and a tiny bit of Yoruba, a language of Nigeria (provided by Kayodè Soyemi). There's also a single line which has been translated into multiple languages via Google Translate (Hindi, Japanese, French, and Spanish). It's possible that those last ones are not the ideal translations, but due to the nature of that line, it's okay if those are wonky.

This is the order of preference of how I would like the play cast/foreign language text handled:

Multilingual— The play is cast with actors of the indicated ethnicities who are able to speak in the languages as indicated in the script. There are no translations. Meanings are transmitted through context and line readings, or not at all. Being uncomfortable by people in power speaking a language you don't understand is part of the point.

Captioned— The play is cast with actors of the indicated ethnicities who are able to speak in the languages as indicated in the script. The non-English language lines are captioned in English.

Accessible— The play is cast with actors of the indicated ethnicities who speak English. They learn to speak a few initial lines of dialogue in the other languages. They then switch to English accompanied by a visual or aural signal that is used to indicate when Chinese or Spanish is being spoken, even as the actors speak in English. Perhaps a sign which lights up that reads "Spanish" or "Chinese", signs that pop up, or a sound or light cue. By this signal we train the audience to recognize when non-English dialogue is being spoken. When the characters "speak" Spanish or Mandarin using English, they speak perfectly well. When Tunde speaks his actual English it is mannered and awkward, but enthusiastic. He knows his English isn't perfect, but has little practice speaking with native speakers. When Russell speaks Spanish she is very poor at it. She halts, struggles for words, and misspeaks, but does the best she can.

This version of the script assumes that the theatre will produce option #1 of the play, with full translation. Previous versions of this script assumed option #3, and can also be chosen for future productions.

The single line of dialogue translated into multiple languages should be rendered into multiple languages and recorded. These can be stilted and imperfect, such as having the automatic reader function of Google Translate read the translated sentence. I have created sound clips in this way and can share them with anyone interested in reading/producing this play. Contact me at greg.lam.writing@gmail.com with any inquiries.

ACT ONE

(At rise, we see the flashing lights of a room of various instruments in action. We hear a voice in the darkness.)

EMERSON: Space…the Final Frontier.

(Lights come up slowly. We see a lone figure seated: Pilot MORRIS EMERSON, a graying space pilot.)

EMERSON: These are the voyages of the Arclight 27.
It's continuing mission:
To haul ass across the galaxy…
Even though we're pretty damn late…
And boldly go where no American has gone before!

(Lights come up to reveal the set, the cockpit of a spaceship, with many lights and indicators and screens showing including an episode of Star Trek. *In contrast to The Enterprise, the ship we're on is shabby, used and worn rather than sleek and impressive.)*

(EMERSON is seated with his feet up, eating a snack and listening to the TV via headphones. He gets up and jams as he warbles the show's theme song.)

EMERSON: Daaa…da da dum…. Da da duuuuummm!
Da da dum dum dum da daa dum…..

(Unheard and unseen by EMERSON, a light flashes and a beep is heard. A computer voice pipes up. It takes some time for him to notice any of this.)

COMPUTER VOICE: *(VO)* Attention! The planet scanned is showing signs of activity. Attention! The planet scanned is showing signs of activity. Attention! The planet scanned is showing—

(EMERSON clambers to the front to look at what's causing the beep. Buttons are pushed. He gets excited.)

EMERSON: O-M-G… *(He presses a button. Into comm)* Addie! Are you outside?

(Offstage we hear a female voice. It is ADDIE RUSSELL.)

RUSSELL: *(OS)* Yeah, fixing the filtration system. You want your water to taste less like my urine, right?

Emerson *(Into comm)* Captain—I have something to report: Holy shit, holy shit, holy shit! And that's official.

RUSSELL: *(OS)* Are you high, Emerson? It's been decades since I've had a joint, and if you—

Emerson *(Into comm)* Just get here, boss. You'll want to see this.

RUSSELL: *(OS)* Fine.

(RUSSELL enters. She is the Captain of the ship. She is similarly dressed, also graying. She holds a tool which she puts away into a wall panel.)

RUSSELL: This better be worth it, Morris.

EMERSON: Lookie there!

RUSSELL: Yes, it's the planet. We saw it hours ago.

EMERSON: No, look! There! LANA[1] found something!

(RUSSELL leans in and looks. She spots it.)

RUSSELL: Are you serious?

---

1   LANA is short for "Logistics And Navigation Assembly", a shorthand name like "Siri" or "Alexa".

EMERSON: Serious as a heart attack. Visual confirmation. When you zoom in you can see it on the screen.

RUSSELL: Those little dots.

EMERSON: Those beautiful dots.

RUSSELL: Light! "Let there be light."

EMERSON: You better believe it. Civilization! They made it! *We* made it! This two thousand year leap of faith is actually going to pay off.

RUSSELL: How far from arrival are we?

EMERSON: Maybe a few hours to get into orbital range.

(Pause. RUSSELL takes in the enormity of the moment.)

EMERSON: You alright, chief?

RUSSELL: Couldn't be better. After two thousand years since The Departure, we will be around for The Arrival.

EMERSON: Hey, we still have to get down there.

RUSSELL: Have they made contact yet?

EMERSON: Not yet.

RUSSELL: Nothing at all?

EMERSON: Nope. No response to any of our hails.

RUSSELL: Strange. They should have a working comm system by now. We should be in range.

EMERSON: I wouldn't worry about it. Those little dots! Lights mean people are living down there. That means we can live down there, too. We'll figure it out.

RUSSELL: Well, Pilot Emerson. Keep sending the hailing signals and stay on course.

EMERSON: "Pilot Emerson?" Really, Addie?

RUSSELL: Yes. I think it's time to start using proper titles around here a little more rigorously.

EMERSON: Why start now?

RUSSELL: We're not alone in the universe anymore. What will the neighbors think?

EMERSON: Right, right. The neighbors. Alright, then. "Captain". Addie. "Captain Addie Russell", sir.

RUSSELL: C'mere, you goof! *(She smiles, goes to* EMERSON, *gives him a strong hug.)* Did you ever think we'd be the ones who actually get to land? All the other crews will be so jealous. They spent their entire lives just minding the ship. But not us!

EMERSON: What did I tell you? Pilot Morris Emerson will get you where you need to go.

RUSSELL: Excited to get on real dirt again?

EMERSON: Yes ma'am! First thing I'm going to do is take a piss, and have honest-to-goodness real gravity pull the stream down to the ground! No more goddamn vacuum system for my junk. It's been twenty-five waking years since I tinkled normally!

RUSSELL: Dream big, Mr Emerson. "One small step for man…"

EMERSON: "One giant leak for mankind!" I can't wait!

*(*EMERSON *and* RUSSELL *laugh.)*

RUSSELL: Oh, before I forget, did you remember to clean out the air filters?

EMERSON: No. Want me to do that now?

RUSSELL: Please. The air quality is at "orange".

EMERSON: Say no more. *(He turns to the side panel and takes out a series of filters and a brush.)* I'll be so happy when this is no longer part of my duties. *(He starts to meticulously brush them clean.)*

RUSSELL: While you're doing that... *(She starts to leave.)*

EMERSON: Where are you going?

RUSSELL: I think it might be time to start bringing some of the upper management out of stasis. Our job is about to be completed. It'll be their turn.

EMERSON: I think we might want to hold off on that.

RUSSELL: Why's that?

EMERSON: According to the protocol manual, the crew on duty has the latitude to determine which passengers need to be revived at any point in time to make use of their particular skills. Right now we don't know whether we need a geologist or a meteorologist or engineer or whatever yet. Let alone a politician, or the military.

RUSSELL: Hm...

EMERSON: Do you disagree?

RUSSELL: Not entirely. Let's be honest. Some of those politicians and military folks are the reason we had to depart Earth in the first place.

EMERSON: Plus it's nice that it's just our ship for a little while longer, isn't it? This place is cramped enough already.

RUSSELL: You have a point. Let's hold off until we finish the surface scans. I'll log in the new developments. *(She goes to a workstation with a microphone and starts recording.)* 12 October, 4240. Eighteen hundred hours. Captain Adelaide Russell reporting. Long range visual scans of the surface of Proxima Centauri B indicate signs of life and civilization on planet surface. We are transmitting our hailing signal and we await our welcome to the established Earth colony. We hope that our next report will be from the surface of our new home.

There we go.

EMERSON: That report, Addie. Straight into history books.

RUSSELL: I know.

EMERSON: This is crazy. This rickety tub has travelled four-point-five light years to get here. That Neptune snafu nearly doomed us, but we made it. Proxima Centauri. Honestly, I wasn't sure we'd ever see it.

RUSSELL: You have to have faith, Emerson. How could our mission fail? I'm in charge!

EMERSON: Yeah, yeah. You're the greatest captain in the universe and all but still... What were the actual odds?

RUSSELL: I'm sure we can revive some statisticians who could calculate the odds for you. I mean, not me. I barely passed Algebra, but one of the geniuses back there...

EMERSON: Hey. None of those eggheads spent the last twenty-five years awake piloting this thing home.

(EMERSON *snaps in the last filter. It beeps.*)

EMERSON: Filter cleaning done.

RUSSELL: Do you ever think about them?

EMERSON: What, the filters? Yeah, I dream about ship maintenance.

RUSSELL: No. Schwartz, and Johannson. Our poor predecessors who'll never live to see the new home. And McGregor and Nielson in stasis before them. And what's their name before them. All of the pilots in deep freeze. Hundreds of dedicated folks who volunteered their lives to help guide this ship.

EMERSON: Won't they all love to get revived?

RUSSELL: Oh my God! We're actually going to meet them! I just realized— We just know them through their reports!

EMERSON: How about those poor bastards who spent their entire lives orbiting Neptune? How many were there? Ten? Craaazy!

RUSSELL: Remember our first day?

EMERSON: How could I forget? Schwartz and Johannson both dying on that spacewalk mishap! And LANA waking us up?

RUSSELL: *(Imitates computer voice)* "Attention! The vital signs of designated crew members have been terminated! In order to ensure a safe arrival, the Arclight failsafe system has revived the next in line to assume command."

EMERSON: *(Imitates computer voice)* "Good morning and welcome back! Analysis shows a debilitating engine problem on the exterior of the craft. As the incoming crew, you have seventy minutes to repair before the craft is compromised."

RUSSELL: Hell of a way to wake up.

EMERSON: But you got out there. Spacewalk, day one. You came through in the clutch. That's when I knew that this chick had the right stuff. When it seemed impossible, you found a way.

RUSSELL: Just doing my job. You know even with all the human ingenuity it took to build this thing, I think the hundreds of human pilots staying sane with only one person to talk to their entire life... That's the real miracle.

EMERSON: You kept me from going crazy all this time. You, all your stories about your sorority, and Netflix.

RUSSELL: Glad to keep such esteemed company. Any signal from the planet yet?

(Pause)

EMERSON: Hold up! LANA's been trying to tell us something.

(EMERSON turns up a dial. We hear a recording. The recording is of a short phrase, spoken over and over. Each time in a different language.)

RECORDING: *(VO. In Hindi)* स्वागत हे। कृपया उस भाषा का नाम बताकर जवाब दें जिसे आप मुख्य रूप से बोलते हैं। Svaagat he. krpaya us bhaasha ka naam bataakar javaab den jise aap mukhy roop se bolate hain.[2]

EMERSON: What the…?

RUSSELL: Ssh. Keep listening.

RECORDING: *(VO. In Chinese)* 欢迎。请以您主要使用的语言回复。 Huānyíng. Qǐng yǐ nín zhǔyào shǐyòng de yǔyán huífù.[3]

EMERSON: Can LANA autotranslate this?

RUSSELL: It's going by too fast.

RECORDING: *(VO. In Japanese)* ようこそ。主に話す言語の名前を言って答えてください。 Yōkoso. Omoni hanasu gengo no namae o itte kotaete kudasai.[4]

RUSSELL: I think that was Japanese…. And Chinese before that.

---

2   [In Hindi: Welcome. Please respond by saying the name of the language that you primarily speak.]

3   [In Chinese: Welcome. Please respond by saying the name of the language that you primarily speak.]

4   [In Japanese: Welcome. Please respond by saying the name of the language that you primarily speak.]

RECORDING: *(VO. In French)* Bienvenue. Veuillez répondre en indiquant le nom de la langue que vous parlez principalement.[5]

EMERSON: French! That was French. "Bien-view?"

RUSSELL: Ssh!

RECORDING: *(VO. In Spanish)* Bienvenido. Favor de responder con el idioma que habla principalmente.[6]

RUSSELL: Spanish! Ugh. They're talking too fast for me.

RECORDING: *(VO. In English)* Welcome. Please respond by saying the name of the language that you primarily speak.

RUSSELL: *(Into Mic)* English! We speak English! American English!

(Pause)

RECORDING: *(VO)* Please hold.

EMERSON: Now what?

RUSSELL: "Please hold", I guess.

EMERSON: Please hold. It's okay. We've been waiting, what? Two thousand years? We can wait a little bit longer…to get to our new home.

RUSSELL: When you say it like that, Morris.

(EMERSON raises an imaginary cup.)

EMERSON: To our new home!

RUSSELL: Here, here! And to Earth! We're sorry we fucked you up. We'll try to do better with this one.

EMERSON: Hey, do you think we'll get a parade?

5   [In French: Welcome. Please respond by saying the name of the language that you primarily speak.]

6   [In Spanish: Welcome. Please respond by saying the name of the language that you primarily speak.]

RUSSELL: What?

EMERSON: A parade! We got sidetracked for so long. They probably thought we were lost for good. "714 Arclights made it! But where's #715?" And now, here we are! The prodigal sons! Blast from the past! They probably thought all hope was gone. a hundred and sixty-five years late! We'll be a miracle.

RUSSELL: I love the way you think. *(Pause)* Still no response?

EMERSON: No.

RUSSELL: I wonder what it's like down there now? They probably arrived at least a century ago. What's happened since then?

EMERSON: Well… If they haven't killed each other by now I think that's a good sign. *(Pause. He looks at his controls.)* So, Addie… You know the thing we were talking about yesterday—

RUSSELL: Not this, again.

EMERSON: I think the situation has changed, hasn't it?

RUSSELL: Why are you so obsessed with this?

EMERSON: I've seen you visit her unit. I know you still care for her.

RUSSELL: Yes, well, I married her.

EMERSON: Okay, fine.

RUSSELL: I also haven't seen her in decades. Look. Carlene is in stasis. Time hasn't moved for her. As far as the universe is concerned, she's twenty-nine years old. She's been twenty-nine years old for two thousand years. That old joke, right? I'm not so lucky.

EMERSON: I just think this might get awkward if we're not on the same page. Do you plan on telling her about us?

RUSSELL: Maybe. Maybe not. I don't know. I've had other things on my mind the past twenty-five years. Who knows? Who knows whether she and I would have stayed together for this long in the best of circumstances? Who knows whether....

EMERSON: What?

RUSSELL: Who knows whether you and I would have happened in any circumstance but this one?

EMERSON: My guess? Probably not.

RUSSELL: Part of me is dreading what comes next. Instead of one person to share your life with there'll be a hundred thousand.... No. More. A hundred thousand plus everyone who's already there. Millions? Billions? It'll be strange being around people again.

EMERSON: I know what you mean...

RUSSELL: How about yourself? You're going to have to relearn how to interact with society pretty soon. Remember that? Small talk?

EMERSON: Oh, geez.

RUSSELL: Friends. Family... Politics.

EMERSON: You know, it's not too late to just steer off course for another fifty years. (Calls out) LANA?

RUSSELL: Come on! We have a duty to fulfill!

EMERSON: Alright, alright. We'll deliver everyone home. Complete our mission, I guess. (Pause) It's just that we're going to have to deal with this eventually—

RUSSELL: Will you stop? I'll deal with this when I'm ready, Okay? Ah, this waiting is driving me nuts. What say we watch something while we wait? Where did we leave off in our *Game of Thrones* rewatch?

EMERSON: I was in the middle of a *Next Generation* marathon, thank you very much.

RUSSELL: Ugh! How do you stand to watch *that* out of all shows? "Computer, go to warp", my ass—

(We hear a different beep coming from the dashboard. EMERSON and RUSSELL notice.)

RUSSELL: We got something!

EMERSON: Patching us through.

(EMERSON presses a button, as he will do whenever they want to communicate.)

EMERSON: *(To CONTROL)* Hello? Can you hear us?

(We hear the offstage voice of CONTROL, the planetary air traffic control equivalent, coming through the ship's comm system.)

CONTROL #1: *(OS)* Approaching vessel, this is Control. Do you read me?

EMERSON: Aw, yeah. Let's go!

EMERSON: *(To CONTROL)* Hello Control! This is Arclight 27. Pilot Morris Emerson reporting. Boy are we glad to hear your voice!

CONTROL #1: *(OS)* Approaching vessel, what is your place of origin?

EMERSON: *(To CONTROL)* We hail from just outside Seattle, Washington.

CONTROL #1: *(OS)* This is a ship from old Earth?

EMERSON: *(To CONTROL)* Yes. Of course. Yes.

CONTROL #1: *(OS)* From the initial launch?

EMERSON: *(TO CONTROL)* Yes.

CONTROL #1: *(OS)* You are from the Great Abandonment?

EMERSON: *(TO CONTROL)* If that's what you call it, yes. I think that's right.

(Pause)

CONTROL #1: *(OS)* And you are from "Washington".
That is of the former United States?

EMERSON: *(To* CONTROL*)* Correct, and proudly so!

CONTROL #1: *(OS)* The, uh, Capitol of United States?

EMERSON: *(To* CONTROL*)* No, "Washington" state. Not
DC. Seattle was a city on the extreme Northwest corner
of the US, in case you forgot.

RUSSELL: Except for Alaska.

EMERSON: I don't think its time for a geography lesson,
Addie.

RUSSELL: Ask them what the weather's like down there!

EMERSON: *(To* CONTROL*)* Control, what's the weather
like down there? We're used to a little rain. *(Pause)*
Hello? Control?

(Pause)

CONTROL #1: *(OS)* You said you were Arclight 27,
correct?

Emerson *(To* CONTROL*)* Yes!

CONTROL #1: *(OS)* What is the payload of your vessel?

EMERSON: *(To* CONTROL*)* Uh…Control, what do you
mean by that?

CONTROL #1: *(OS)* Personnel, resources, reserves.
What's your inventory?

EMERSON: *(To* CONTROL*)* There are…just over a
hundred thousand people in stasis on board. We have
enough resources for—

RUSSELL: Tell them a month. *(Pause)* I don't want to
wait, do you?

EMERSON: *(To* CONTROL*)* —About a month before this
vessel becomes nonviable.

(Pause)

CONTROL #1: *(OS)* Please hold.

EMERSON: Not exactly the warmest welcome, wouldn't you say? No "congratulations!" or anything?

RUSSELL: We weren't exactly expected I think. I bet they're trying to figure out where we should land. Who knows what the state of their airports are?

EMERSON: You'd think there'd be some sort of welcome wagon.

RUSSELL: Just be patient. There's a process, right? There's a process to everything.

EMERSON: Okay. I'm sure you're right.

CONTROL #1: *(OS)* Arclight 27? Do you read me?

EMERSON: *(To* CONTROL*)* Yes, yes we do.

CONTROL #1: *(OS)* Apologies for the delay. We're sending you a flight path. Let me know when you receive it.

*(*RUSSELL *checks the instruments.)*

RUSSELL: Got it.

EMERSON: *(To* CONTROL*)* We have received it.

CONTROL #1: *(OS)* Good. Please input that flight path to your system and wait for further instruction.

*(*EMERSON *inputs the information in. He looks puzzled.)*

EMERSON: *(To* CONTROL*)* Control? This flight path seems to be a simple orbit around the planet.

CONTROL #1: *(OS)* That is correct. Is it in your system?

EMERSON: *(To* CONTROL*)* Yes, but we thought we'd receive instructions on where and how to land on the planet.

CONTROL #1: *(OS)* That is yet to be determined. Right now we need you to input the path into your system. Can you confirm?

EMERSON: *(To* CONTROL*)* Yes, we're on it. But the ultimate destination. That's forthcoming, right? And the timetable?

(Pause)

CONTROL #1: *(OS)* Stay on that path. Please hold.

EMERSON: *(To* CONTROL*)* Control! Do you read me? We just need to know— Control!

RUSSELL: What is going on?

EMERSON: They're sandbagging us.

RUSSELL: *(To* CONTROL*)* Control, this is the Captain speaking. We are rather eager to find out if there's a protocol for arrival that has been established. If that's the case, we will work closely with you to follow those protocols.

(Pause. They listen.)

RUSSELL: Nothing.

CONTROL #1: *(OS)* Arclight 27, you are aware that you have been significantly delayed from the previous Arclights? Please confirm.

RUSSELL: *(To* CONTROL*)* Yes, according to our logs we had an incident that required us to stay in the orbit of Neptune for repairs for one of its solar revolutions before we could continue. That delayed us around a hundred and sixty-five years. We're lucky to have made it at all.

CONTROL #1: *(OS)* There are a number of issues we must discuss.

RUSSELL: *(To* CONTROL*)* Well, we're happy to discuss them.

CONTROL #1: *(OS)* You misunderstand, Captain. The discussion is not with you but amongst ourselves.

RUSSELL: *(To* CONTROL*)* Could we have an idea of what sort of—

CONTROL #1: *(OS)* Please hold.

RUSSELL: *(To* CONTROL*)* No, don't— *(To* EMERSON*)* Son of a bitch. Why can't we get a straight answer?

EMERSON: We gotta land.

RUSSELL: I know.

EMERSON: We're so close. It's a miracle this crate has lasted this long. It's more duct tape than anything else at this point.

RUSSELL: Is there any place on the surface that looks like a potential landing spot?

EMERSON: Are we assuming that the current residents are hostile?

RUSSELL: I'm not making any assumptions at this point. But I want to make sure we have options.

EMERSON: I'll scan the topography of the surface and come up with a few candidates.

RUSSELL: Good. I'll see if I can find out if there's a geologist we can—

CONTROL #1: *(OS)* Arclight 27!

EMERSON: Crap. *(To* CONTROL*)* Yes?

CONTROL #1: *(OS)* Arclight 27? What would you say is the genetic makeup of your ship's payload?

EMERSON: *(To* CONTROL*)* I beg your pardon?

CONTROL #1: *(OS)* The hundred thousand people on your ship that you claimed. What percentage is Caucasian in origin, African, Asian, etc.?

EMERSON: *(To* CONTROL*)* Control, I fail to see how that's relevant.

(Pause)

RUSSELL: What is this?

CONTROL #1: *(OS)* Arclight 27, can you answer our question?

EMERSON: *(To* CONTROL*)* Control, I'm struggling to see the relevance of the question.

(Pause)

CONTROL #1: *(OS)* We require an answer to the question.

EMERSON: *(To* CONTROL*)* Not until we get an answer to what's going on. Why is that necessary information?

CONTROL #1: *(OS)* We just need. Some background. On the origins of the people on your vessel. It's just standard procedure.

EMERSON: *(To* CONTROL*)* We're Americans. From Seattle. What does it matter our "genetic background"?

CONTROL #1: *(OS)* You refuse to furnish us with that information?

EMERSON: *(To* CONTROL*)* We really need to know why you're asking. It's a disturbing line of questioning.

(Pause)

CONTROL #1: *(OS)* Please hold.

EMERSON: *(To* CONTROL*)* No! No! Don't— *(To* RUSSELL*)* Again! *(Pause)* You agree, right? Or should we tell them?

RUSSELL: With you completely. Not until they tell us why.

EMERSON: Addie. Look down here.

*(*EMERSON *points to a screen.* RUSSELL *looks.)*

RUSSELL: Okay. Looks like land.

EMERSON: Most of the energy activity in this landmass is concentrated on the Northern coast. This part down South looks both pretty flat and unoccupied. It could do in a pinch.

RUSSELL: Put a pin in it. Let's hope we don't need to resort to crashing the party.

(CONTROL *pops up again. This time it's a different voice,* CONTROL 2.)

CONTROL #2: *(OS)* Hello out there! Arclight 27! Do you read me? This is Control.

EMERSON: *(To* CONTROL*)* We read you Control. You sound a little different.

CONTROL #2: *(OS)* Yes. My name is Manisha. How are you doing today?

Emerson *(TO* CONTROL*)* Good. I think. Honestly, Manoosha, we're a little concerned that we have yet to receive a timetable as to when we may be able to land and complete our mission.

CONTROL #2: *(OS)* Arclight 27, I understand your concern, and I share it. Before we can determine whether you'll be allowed to land on *Yeni Dünya*[7], we must find out more about who is on your ship.

EMERSON: *(To* CONTROL*)* Control, I'm not sure we heard what you said correctly. Could you repeat? "Yeni"…?

CONTROL #2: *(OS)* I said: before we determine whether you'll be allowed to land on the planet we need some more information. We appreciate your patience in this matter.

_____

7   Turkish for "New World", what the Proximans call the planet.

EMERSON: *(To* CONTROL*)* "Allowed?" What— Why
wouldn't we be allowed to land on the planet?

CONTROL #2: *(OS)* Please remain calm, sir.

EMERSON: *(To* CONTROL*)* I am very calm. What is the
reason you wouldn't allow us to land on the planet?
If it's something like possible germs we could be
quarantined for—

CONTROL #2: *(OS)* More basic than that. We need to
know what is the makeup of the people on your ship.
How many whites, how many blacks, how many
others. You know. It's a simple question.

EMERSON: *(To* CONTROL*)* It's an irrelevant question.

(Pause)

CONTROL #2: *(OS)* Here's something that crossed our
minds. What was the name of the ship that landed on
your home continent and met your Indians? The flower
ship?

EMERSON: *(To* CONTROL*)* You mean the Mayflower?
Plymouth Rock? And we called them Native
Americans, actually.

CONTROL #2: *(OS)* Yes, them. How were the Europeans
on that ship received?

EMERSON: *(To* CONTROL*)* Pretty well if I remember my
history right. They had Thanksgiving and everything.

CONTROL #2: *(OS)* Yes. And how did they end up? The
Europeans and the Natives of America? Equitable?

EMERSON: *(To* CONTROL*)* You know a lot of time has
passed since that all went down.

CONTROL #2: *(OS)* How did the African peoples fare
upon first meeting the Europeans? The Asian people
have some stories, too.

RUSSELL: *(To* CONTROL*)* Control, do you read me? This is Captain Adelaide Russell.

CONTROL #2: *(OS)* This is Control. I am Manisha. We hear you, Captain.

RUSSELL: *(To* CONTROL*)* Great, Manisha. Now we have requested permission to land on the planet. By the terms of the International Interplanetary Exploration Compact, agreed to by all parties who were able to successfully launch Arc ships, you must grant us that right. *(Pause. To* CONTROL*)* Hello? Control. Please answer.

CONTROL #2: *(OS)* The compact…that you speak of. It was a long time ago.

RUSSELL: *(To* CONTROL*)* Everyone agreed to it.

CONTROL #2: *(OS)* It has since been superceded by many Constitutional agreements that were formed in the years after planetary foundation. The compact is no longer valid.

EMERSON: Jesus Christ…

RUSSELL: *(To* CONTROL*)* Well, can we discuss this after we safely land our vessel? We have over one hundred thousand lives, men, women and children that are depending on safe passage here. The detour we were forced to undergo cost us a lot of time and resources. We won't be able to seek another habitable planet.

CONTROL #2: *(OS)* We are aware of your situation. It is very difficult.

RUSSELL: *(To* CONTROL*)* Then let us land.

CONTROL #2: *(OS)* We cannot grant permission at this time. We ask you to be patient. We are doing the best that we can.

RUSSELL: *(To* CONTROL*)* Why not?!

CONTROL #2: *(OS)* We require you to maintain an orbit around our planet until further instruction is given.

RUSSELL: *(To* CONTROL*)* This is not an acceptable response. We have every right to land on the planet as you did when you arrived.

CONTROL #2: *(OS)* We are unable to grant you permission at this time.

RUSSELL: *(To* CONTROL*)* Give us a reason, Control! We demand you give us a reason!

CONTROL #2: *(OS)* You remember that we asked you a question as to the demographic makeup of the passengers of your vessel.

RUSSELL: *(To* CONTROL*)* Why is that relevant?

CONTROL #2: *(OS)* According to our records, at the time of the departure, the United States were said to have upwards of sixty percent of people with a Caucasian background, around twelve percent African, five percent Asian, ten percent Latino, and some others. Is that also the makeup of your vessel?

RUSSELL: *(To* CONTROL*)* If you must know, it's probably more like eighty percent white. Seattle wasn't the most diverse part of the Union... At least the people who could actually get on this ship. But we're good people. See, we try not to see color.

CONTROL #2: *(OS)* I see. Then there you have it.

*(*RUSSELL *and* EMERSON *look at each other.)*

RUSSELL: *(To* CONTROL*)* What? What do we have?

CONTROL #2: *(OS)* Your ship contains eighty percent Americans of European heritage. On *Yeni Dünya* where we value peace and equality above all, we are not sure that we are able to welcome a people with such a known malicious and destructive history as yours.

(EMERSON *explodes.* RUSSELL *tries to calm him. Their lines can overlap.*)

EMERSON: *(To* CONTROL*)* Are you fucking kidding me!?

RUSSELL: Morris!

EMERSON: *(To* CONTROL*)* You're not letting us down there because we're white?! Who do you think you are? Who the fuck do you think you are?

RUSSELL: Morris! Calm down. This doesn't help.

EMERSON: *(To* CONTROL*)* America was the greatest country we had, you little asshole.

CONTROL #2: *(OS)* Sir! Excuse me…Sir!

RUSSELL: I'm shutting down your mic.

EMERSON: *(To* CONTROL*)* Where were you from? I guarantee we saved your ass somewhere down the line. Or kicked it! Or both!

RUSSELL: Stand down! That's an order!

(Pause)

CONTROL #2: *(OS)* I see that we have upset you. That was not our intent.

RUSSELL: *(To* CONTROL*)* Control, your stated reasons are misguided at best. This is a peaceful mission of exploration and resettlement, the same mission your ancestors signed off on over two thousand years ago. No one is seeking to harm anyone.

(Pause)

RUSSELL: Hello? Did you hear—?

EMERSON: They stiffed us again.

RUSSELL: Can you put us in position to make a reentry?

EMERSON: Yes. If that's what you want to do.

RUSSELL: Don't tip our hand but look at that plateau and find us landing spots. I want to try to talk with them one more time. Maybe get some back up. There's gotta be someone in here smarter than us.

EMERSON: C'mon! Don't do that. The self-deprecation act. You know you're a badass. If there's a way… You'll find it.

(CONTROL *pipes up again. This time with the original voice.*)

CONTROL #1: *(OS)* Arclight 27. Do you read me?

EMERSON: *(OS)* Yes. We're back to you, now? We were kind of liking "Mashuna-Matata" better.

CONTROL #1: *(OS)* She has told you too much. We have several options for you. You will choose one of them.

EMERSON: *(To* CONTROL*)* I'm sure we'll love all of them.

CONTROL #1: *(OS)* Option one. We will send supplies up to you that will allow you to extend your stay in orbit. That will give us time to hold a worldwide referendum on allowing you to land.

(EMERSON *and* RUSSELL *look at each other.*)

EMERSON: *(To* CONTROL*)* I don't think—

CONTROL #1: *(OS)* I have not finished. Option two. We agree to allow any of your passengers of the age ten years or younger to board shuttles that we will send to you. They will be fostered by families on the ground while we take control of your ship.

EMERSON: *(To* CONTROL*)* Just the kids? Just the kids? Are you insane? What about us adults?

CONTROL #1: *(OS)* That would be determined at a later date. The adults would remain in stasis until determination is made. The next option—

RUSSELL: *(To* CONTROL*)* Control, we need to speak to your president, or prime minister. Whatever you've got going on. "Take me to your leader", I guess.

CONTROL #1: *(OS)* We have not finished going over the options.

RUSSELL: *(To* CONTROL*)* With all due respect, we don't find these options or anything like these options to be remotely acceptable. We demand to speak to your leadership as soon as possible. Is there an American embassy?

CONTROL #1: *(OS)* Embassy? Of course not!

RUSSELL: *(To* CONTROL*)* What does that mean?

(Pause)

CONTROL #1: *(OS)* We'll see what we can arrange. Until then, stay on your designated flight path. We will contact you when we have more to tell you. Control out.

EMERSON: Unbelievable! What's their problem?

RUSSELL: I don't know, but I'm done trying to talk to them. Prepare for a solo reentry. We'll crash this thing if necessary. Scout out any defenses, threats, satellites. Who knows what they have?

EMERSON: Good. Screw them. Fucking assholes.

*(*RUSSELL *starts to exit)*

EMERSON: Where are you going?

RUSSELL: We have to get someone.

EMERSON: Right. Let's revive the military guys.

RUSSELL: No. Not military. They'd just going to have the same conversation we had. And we have nothing to threaten with, do we? They didn't outfit this ship with weapons that can hurt a planet. We don't have anything more threatening than riot gear. Who knows

what they have? We don't need military. We need
diplomacy. We need a diplomat that can speak their
language and talk our way out of this.

EMERSON: Who would that be? We're not exactly
Washington DC! We don't have Thinktank brains and
speechwriters. We do have fifteen thousand software
engineers if you want them.

RUSSELL: Let me look at the manifest. There has to be
someone.

(EMERSON *nods.* RUSSELL *exits. Lights fade.*)

Scene: Henry's revival

(*A large screen lights up in the middle of stage. A
friendly UI element comes up. Perhaps an animated logo
like Microsoft's "Clippy". Or a text-based powerpoint
presentation. Or nature slides. In any case, there is a
very chipper voice that is heard that matches with the
presentation. The* VOICE *is friendly and professional.*)

VOICE: (*VO*) Good afternoon! We have some good
news for you today! To continue in English, select "1"!
¡Buenas dias! ¡Tenemos buenas noticias para ti hoy!
Para continuar en *Español*, selecc—

(*A beep is heard.*)

VOICE: (*VO*) The day we have all been waiting for,
Arrival Day, is imminent. Arclight 27 is approximately
[splice] seven hours [/splice] from arriving at our
destination, Proxima Centauri B. In anticipation,
you have been revived and we are glad to help you
receive orientation in this exciting new phase in human
existence.

(*Pause*)

VOICE: *(VO)* Your crew will be releasing you from your stasis pod momentarily. Please do not try to move, as your muscles may have atrophied from [splice] 2,193 years [/splice] of inactivity. Please follow the crew's instructions, as disobeying an order from a crew member is a crime punishable by immediate death without warning or trial. While you wait, would you like a beverage? Press "1" for coffee. Press "2" for—

(A beep is heard.)

VOICE: *(VO)* Arclight 27 is proud to present you with Starbucks Coffee. Due to the limitations of space travel, we can only offer you coffee at room temperature with milk substitute and corn syrup. Please enjoy!

(In the darkness, a human's voice can be heard. It is HENRY HIRANO *[25]. He has just been revived.)*

HENRY: *(VO)* Hello?

VOICE: *(VO)* Please relax as we show you a short featurette about the making of Arclight 27, narrated by Morgan Freeman.

HENRY: *(VO)* Can someone get me out of here?

(Generic music plays. The sound of a fist knocking on metal is heard.)

HENRY: *(VO)* Hello? Is anyone real outside? Hello?

MORGAN FREEMAN: *(VO)* A world in environmental crisis…. Air…unbreathable… Cities…in ruin. Oceans…

HENRY: *(VO)* Can someone get me out of this thing!?!

Scene: Bridge

(Lights come on. We see RUSSELL *helping* HENRY HIRANO *onto the bridge.* HENRY *has his head hung down and is struggling physically. He wears a preservation suit with*

*some sort of helmet which obscures some of his facial
features.)*

RUSSELL: There we go, sir. There we go. That's it. One
foot and then the other. It'll come back to you.

HENRY: Feeling pretty nauseous right now.

RUSSELL: That's to be expected. You've been in stasis
for a few millenia.

EMERSON: Well, hello to the new guy! First new face
around here in years. I'm Morris. Morris Emerson.

HENRY: Hi. I'm Henry.

RUSSELL: Mr Hirano is just getting reacclimated, aren't
you?

HENRY: I feel kinda sick. Might puke up that coffee I
just had.

EMERSON: Oh, God. Did you actually drink that? Well,
we have space sickness bags if you need it. Just let us
know.

HENRY: I thought we weren't going to be revived until
we reached the surface.

RUSSELL: Well, that was the plan but we seem to have
run into a bit of a situation here, sir.

HENRY: Call me Henry.

RUSSELL: Right, Henry.

HENRY: And what was your name again?

RUSSELL: Addie. Captain Adelaide Russell.

HENRY: Adelaide Russell. Do I know you? Your name
sounds familiar.

RUSSELL: Uh, we were discussing the situation at hand,
Mr Hirano.

HENRY: Oh, right. The situation. What situation?

RUSSELL: Well, sir. As we approached Proxima Centauri B to begin to plan our descent, we discovered that the previous arclights… Well, we should mention that we were delayed for quite some time. A hundred and sixty-five years.

HENRY: A hundred and sixty-five years?!

RUSSELL: Our predecessors reported an incident around Neptune. A disturbance led to a collision which- That's not important right now. The thing is that we have been rebuffed by the planet's established inhabitants when we have requested permission to land at our destination despite the international compact all nations agreed to.

HENRY: Really?

EMERSON: These jerkwads hate America or something.

RUSSELL: Morris, not now.

HENRY: That sucks. What are you going to do about it?

RUSSELL: Well, sir—

HENRY: Henry.

RUSSELL: Henry. We hoped that you'd be able to lend us your legal and negotiation expertise to help ameliorate our situation.

HENRY: My…expertise?

RUSSELL: Yes. We checked our manifest and thought your combination of twenty-seven years as a sitting judge and also teaching international contract law would be beneficial. Not to mention your brief time as ambassador to South Korea.

HENRY: Oh, no. I—

EMERSON: Also, you're one of *them*.

HENRY: One of-?

RUSSELL: What Pilot Emerson means is that the people who have established the colony on Proxima Centauri seem to be a…little obsessed with ethnicity. They keep asking about us the racial makeup of the ship. And they don't seem to be of a mind to be charitable towards…people like us.

EMERSON: Bunch of ingrates.

RUSSELL: Not now, Morris.

HENRY: Quick question: Who's "us"?

RUSSELL: Pardon?

HENRY: When you say "people like us", who does "us" mean?

RUSSELL: I don't know, exactly. Americans? White people? Seahawks fans? Who's to say? Our conversations with them have not been productive so far.

HENRY: Right. Okay. So one thing. When you say that I have twenty-seven years of experience on the bench and a teaching career…I actually don't.

RUSSELL: You don't? But…Mr Hirano. Your files—

HENRY: Right. My files. Those are actually my father's files. Henry Hirano, *Senior*. He… He gave up his spot on the ship for me. *(He removes his helmet. He's not old enough to have had the described career.)* I'm Henry Hirano, *Junior*. I…I am, or *was*, getting my law degree at U-Dub. I was one year away from graduation… if there are any law schools down there that accept transfer credit, I'd love to talk with them.

(Pause)

EMERSON: Fuck!

RUSSELL: You lied? You boarded this vessel illegally?

HENRY: It was my pop's idea! He was like: "I'm sixty-five years old. What am I going to do on a new planet? You're young, you should have that chance." And I got in. It was a pretty hectic scene, if you recall. Apparently he pulled enough strings to get me in.

RUSSELL: Jesus Christ! This is Stanford all over again.

HENRY: Wait, Stanford? What do—

EMERSON: You jumped the line, huh? That's just great. I was the only one of my family who got a spot on the Arc even though I'm a pilot. I didn't have enough "pull" to get any of my pals aboard. But I'm so glad your dad did. (To RUSSELL) Permission to kick his ass out of the airlock, Captain.

RUSSELL: Permission denied, Emerson. Mr Hirano, your foolish actions may have jeopardized the lives of a hundred thousand people on this ship. We are in desperate need of a knowledgeable expert to help guide us in a dire situation, and instead we have... you.

HENRY: Look, guys. I'm sorry. I had no idea. But maybe I could help. I did get a B+ in Contract Theory.

EMERSON: Addie, let's go find someone else. Dump him back into deep freeze and—

(An alarm sounds.)

HENRY: What is that?

EMERSON: LANA, talk to me.

COMPUTER VOICE: (VO) Attention! Incoming vessel approaching! Attention! Incoming—

(The three race towards the controls. EMERSON shuts off the warning.)

EMERSON: Something is heading towards us. A... spaceship?

RUSSELL: Is it hostile?

EMERSON: I don't think so. It's tiny, like 3 meters across. No visible weapons. A personal shuttle? Maybe they're sending an envoy to greet us?

RUSSELL: Hail them.

EMERSON: *(To spacecraft)* Incoming craft. This is Arclight 27. Please identify yourself.

(Pause. No answer)

EMERSON: Nothing.

RUSSELL: Try again. All frequencies.

EMERSON: Incoming craft. This is Arclight 27. Incoming— It's heading right at us! Speeding up!

RUSSELL: Evasive maneuvers!

(EMERSON steers hard. The actors react. The sound of a collision)

EMERSON: It hit us! Jesus Christ!

RUSSELL: Where is it?

EMERSON: Destroyed. Like a…Smartcar hitting a cruise ship. The hull is okay, but we got lucky.

RUSSELL: I didn't see a pilot. I think it was unmanned, sent to crash into us.

EMERSON: A real kamikaze mission. *(To* HENRY*)* No offense, Henry.

HENRY: They're throwing cars at us?

EMERSON: Unmanned space shuttles.

RUSSELL: Why? We were following their flightpath.

EMERSON: Well, actually…

RUSSELL: Emerson! I told you to maintain orbit!

EMERSON: I…just let it drift a touch to the Southern hemisphere to get another look at that landing site.

RUSSELL: We should course correct and return to the orbital path.

EMERSON: What?

RUSSELL: Get out of immediate danger and try to talk to them.

EMERSON: They shot an Uber at us! They don't want to talk.

RUSSELL: We strayed from orbit. We have to tell them it was unintentional.

EMERSON: But—

RUSSELL: Enough. We open a line to Control. That's a command. And we're going to talk about this later.

(With a sigh, EMERSON *opens a communication line.)*

EMERSON: All yours.

RUSSELL: *(To* CONTROL*)* Arclight 27 to Control. What is the meaning of the craft that just strafed our ship?

CONTROL #1: *(OS)* Arclight 27, you were instructed to maintain orbit around the planet. Instead your flight path has deviated from our instructions.

RUSSELL: *(To* CONTROL*)* So you shot a projectile at an unarmed vessel without warning? Endangering the lives of a hundred thousand people? There are children on board!

CONTROL #1: *(OS)* It was you who jeopardized those lives by not obeying orders. Return to the specified orbit immediately.

RUSSELL: *(To* CONTROL*)* That was a pilot error which will be corrected. But we insist upon a firm timetable for landing this vessel.

CONTROL #1: *(OS)* We have not determined that you have the right—

RUSSELL: *(To* CONTROL*)* Of course we have the right. We all had equal settlement rights when we left Earth. We agreed on this in the Compact. Shooting at us is an act of war.

CONTROL #1: *(OS)* What gives you the right to the hundrd and sixty-five years of hard won progress in our taming of this world? You who have contributed nothing but you want to reap the rewards? You now expect equal voice in our decisions?

RUSSELL: *(To* CONTROL*)* Can we land and then discuss this?

CONTROL #1: *(OS)* You are to return to the orbit that we specified for you. Any unauthorized attempt to land will result in further defensive measures taken against your vessel.

RUSSELL: *(To* CONTROL*)* We are seeking asylum!

CONTROL #1: *(OS)* Asylum has not been granted.

EMERSON: Addie! More bogeys are coming our way!

RUSSELL: Evasive action!

*(*EMERSON *steers, the passengers recoil. Another collision happens.)*

HENRY: Jesus!

RUSSELL: They're actually trying to kill us.

EMERSON: Hull is still holding for now. Permission to take this thing down!

HENRY: What? Fly *into* all that?

EMERSON: It's that or die out here. If they're flinging vehicles at us, that means they don't have missiles or lasers, right? Once we start reentering they can't stop us!

RUSSELL: We don't know that. We have enough provisions for a while if we can get them to stop hurling crap at us.

EMERSON: Do you really think they'll change their minds?

HENRY: We have to try talking to them!

EMERSON: Oh, really? Was there a course at U-Dub that covered this situation, professor?

RUSSELL: Maintain orbit, Emerson. We will try to talk first. Let's find another scholar who can talk to them.

EMERSON: But what if we get another stowaway like this jerk?

HENRY: Hey! I'm not to blame here.

RUSSELL: I'm sorry, Mr Hirano. Mr Emerson is right in that we—

EMERSON: Incoming!

(Another collision)

EMERSON: From the rear! Sneaky bastards. Still holding.

RUSSELL: *(To* CONTROL*)* Control. You are firing on an unarmed vessel containing a hundred thousand innocent civilians! We are in the process of correcting our orbit!

CONTROL #1: *(OS)* We require you to move to the specified flightpath immediately!

RUSSELL: *(To* CONTROL*)* Can we discuss this? We have…a legal expert. Dr Henry Hirano. Of the prestigious University of Washington.

HENRY: What are you—

RUSSELL: Just play along. *(To* CONTROL*)* Dr Hirano has some thoughts about the…issues involved.

HENRY: *(To* CONTROL*)* Um. Hello. Good to...speak with you today. It, uh...seems to me that we are in the position of classic asylum seekers, and as such we are entitled to certain protections—

CONTROL #1: *(OS)* What is your last name again?

HENRY: *(To* CONTROL*)* Hirano.

CONTROL #1: *(OS)* Is that Spanish? Your name?

HENRY: *(To* CONTROL*)* Uh, Japanese in origin. *(To others)* Why are they asking that?

RUSSELL: They seem to favor some ethnicities.

EMERSON: They're fucking racists.

HENRY: *(To* CONTROL*)* As I was saying, asylum seeking has a long history in—

CONTROL #1: *(OS)* How do they treat you, Dr Hirano?

HENRY: *(To* CONTROL*)* Excuse me?

CONTROL #1: *(OS)* Your colleagues. They are both white, right? Do they treat you like equals? With respect?

HENRY: *(To* CONTROL*)* I've...I've only just met them. But no complaints so far.

CONTROL #1: *(OS)* We've heard so many stories.

HENRY: *(To* CONTROL*)* Like anyone there's some good and some bad but on the whole they don't seem that bad.

CONTROL #1: *(OS)* Interesting.

EMERSON: "Not that bad"?! We're fighting for our lives, here, chump!

HENRY: I don't want to oversell it.

EMERSON: They're firing space junk at us!

RUSSELL: Morris. Enough! *(To* HENRY*)* A little more salesmanship might be in order, "Dr Hirano".

CONTROL #1: *(OS)* Dr Hirano!

HENRY: *(To* CONTROL*)* Yes! Yes!

CONTROL #1: *(OS)* We will not deploy more deterrents upon you now, but we need you to maintain orbit. Await further instructions.

HENRY: *(To* CONTROL*)* Understood. Have a great day!

RUSSELL: That's something at least. A little breathing room. Let's try to keep our wits about us, gentlemen. We have time now, we can go back and find someone in the back to help us strategize. Mr Emerson, bring us to—

(A warning beep is heard.)

EMERSON: Oh, no. Oh, no, oh, no. *(He feverishly checks his instruments.)*

RUSSELL: What?

EMERSON: The last collision. I think it damaged our life support. The oxygen levels are dropping.

RUSSELL: No.

EMERSON: We have to land. We have to land *now*.

RUSSELL: How much time?

EMERSON: I don't know. Four hours? Tops!

HENRY: Maybe we can get them—

RUSSELL: No. Enough talk.

EMERSON: Finally!

HENRY: No! Captain Russell—

(RUSSELL sits in her seat and straps in.)

RUSSELL: The decision is made for us. We didn't come halfway across the galaxy to die on the doorstep. I have a ship full of people to protect. We're going in.

HENRY: But— But—

RUSSELL: Emerson! Bring us down, any way you can. If you see a good landing site, get us there.

EMERSON: Copy that.

HENRY: Shit. Shit.

RUSSELL: I'd suggest—

HENRY: Yes, Yes! I know! Where's my helmet?

EMERSON: Changing course now.

(The actors lurch at the change in direction.)

RUSSELL: Lord forgive us if this goes wrong.

CONTROL #1: *(OS)* Arclight 27! You have begun an unauthorized descent! Abort at once or—

RUSSELL: *(To* CONTROL*)* Negative. We have a critical life support failure on board caused by your latest round of projectiles. We must get on ground now.

CONTROL #1: *(OS)* It was your failure to follow our protocols that led us to attack—

RUSSELL: Turn them down.

EMERSON: With pleasure.

*(*EMERSON *lowers the volume on* CONTROL, *rendering them almost inaudible. The remainder of* CONTROL'*s faint dialogue is in the footnote below.[8])*

HENRY: This is insane. The future is insane. *(He sits and starts to strap in.)*

EMERSON: Strap in! I'm gonna take her down.

RUSSELL: Make it so, pilot.

(Everyone's dialogue overlaps [pages 38 & 39 together]:)

------

8   [—If you had followed our instructions from the start, you would not be in this situation... Hello? ...Are you listening? ...I think...I think that they cut us off... Yes, I'll keep trying. What's this? ...They— ...What are they...? They are entering without permission! Look! ...Yes, I will.]

EMERSON:	RUSSELL:	HENRY:
Navigation, check. Hull integrity, check. Systems are a go. Hold onto your helmets, everyone. *(He steers.)*	I need to log this.	
		Are we…
Ready or not, here we come!	It might be our last chance.	
		Are we sure we want to do this?
	(Into recording)	
We are reaching the upper atmosphere in ten seconds. Hull holding steady!	12 October, 4240. Twenty-one hundred hours. Captain Adelaide Russell reporting.	Oh, God! "Take my place, son. You have your whole life ahead of you…"
There are more unmanned craft on the way. We will outrun them.	We have been fired upon by Proximans! Unprovoked. It has damaged our ship. Repeat: We have been damaged! We are attempting—	What are we doing? What are we doing?
Hull temperatures are climbing! If anyone knows any prayers, now's the time to say them….		Holy shit! Holy fucking shit!
		I DON'T LIKE THE FUTURE!

COMPUTER VOICE: *(VO)*	CONTROL
	(Audible again)
Attention! The ship is entering planetary atmosphere! Please be sure to be seated and securely fastened.	Arclight 27. You are making an unauthorized entry.
	Turn around immediately You are making an unauthorized
Re-entry can have an extreme amount of turbulence	entry.
	Turn around immediately. You will be
Attention! The ship is entering planetary atmosphere…	turned away by force, if necessary.

(The stage lights up in a blaze of red. Blackout)

END OF ACT ONE

ACT TWO

(At rise, we see the same control room as in ACT ONE, but disheveled, aslant, and empty. The ship has crash-landed, and debris is everywhere. One entire window is smashed open. Sunlight streams in. Power is down on instruments except for the TV.)

(We hear an alarm and the sound of the COMPUTER VOICE *repeating a phrase.)*

COMPUTER VOICE: *(VO)* Attention! We have come to an emergency landing. Please follow the lights to the nearest exit! A crew member will find you and assist you. Attention! We have come to an emergency landing....

(The sound of breathing from behind a gas mask is heard. Ominous)

(We hear the sound of footsteps, and one voice talking to another. The first voice is TUNDE *[Toon-day], a security officer. He speaks in Mandarin Chinese.)*

TUNDE: *(OS)* 啊！ 我应该能把那该死的警报关掉了。A! Wǒ yīnggāi néng bǎ nà gāisǐ de jǐngbào guān diàole.[9]

(We see/hear a hand clicking on a keypad. The alarm and announcement abruptly stop.)

TUNDE: *(OS)* 终于！ 安静一点了。Zhōngyú! Ānjìng yīdiǎnle.[10] *(He pries open the door and enters. He wears a*

---

9 Aha! I think I can shut off that damn alarm.

10 Finally! Be quiet.

protective uniform. He's armed with a gun. He looks at the instruments.)

TUNDE: *(To* COMM*)* Paz，我在舰桥上了。测量设备显示空气质量很安全，所以我要把头盔拿掉了。Paz, wǒ zài jiàn qiáo shàngle. Cèliáng shèbèi xiǎnshì kōngqì zhì liàng hěn ānquán, suǒyǐ wǒ yào bǎ tóukuī ná diàole.[11]

(We hear the voice of PAZ*, another officer. She also speaks Mandarin.)*

PAZ: *(OS)* 小心点。Xiǎoxīn diǎn.[12]

*(*TUNDE *takes off his helmet, revealing his face. His ethnicity is largely African. He looks to a panel on the side. Over the next line, static is heard over the comm system.)*

TUNDE: *(To* COMM*)* 好多了。Paz，这些美国人真的摧毁了这个舰桥。没有尸体。他们一定逃走了。Hǎoduōle. Paz, zhèxiē měiguó rén zhēn de cuīhuǐle zhègè jiàn qiáo. Méiyǒu shītǐ. Tāmen yīdìng táozǒule.[13]

PAZ: *(OS)* 那你把枪准备好。Nà nǐ bǎ qiāng zhǔnbèi hǎo.[14] *¡Cuidado!*[15]

TUNDE: *(To* COMM*)* 我在! 我在! Wǒ zài! Wǒ zài![16] *(He looks around. To* COMM*)* 电源还开着, 但是自动系统好像下线了。原生舱情况如何? Diànyuán hái kāizhe, dànshì zìdòng xìtǒng hǎoxiàng xià xiànle. Yuánshēng cāng qíngkuàng rúhé?[17]

---

11 Paz, I'm on the bridge. Readings say the air quality is safe. I'm taking off my helmet.

12 Be careful.

13 Much better. Paz, these Americans really destroyed this bridge. I don't see bodies. They must have escaped.

14 Then have your gun ready.

15 Careful!

16 Yes, yes.

17 The power is still on, but the automatic systems seems to be offline. What is the status of the stasis pods?

PAZ: *(OS)* 还在运转中。他们都还睡着, 感谢创建者。Hái
zài yùn zhuǎn zhōng. Tāmen dōu hái shuìzhe, gǎnxiè
chuàngjiàn zhě.[18]

TUNDE: *(To* COMM*)* 哇! ¡Dios mío! 你看这个! Wa! ¡Dios
mío! Nǐ kàn zhège![19]

PAZ: *(OS)* 什么? 那是什么? Shénme? Nà shì shénme cí?[20]

TUNDE: *(To* COMM*)* 他们的娱乐设备还可以用呢! 我看看...有
"Netflix"! "Disney Plus"! 还有个 "Hulu"。 "Hulu"
是什么? 这真是太神奇了! 有HBO吗? Tāmen de yúlè shèbèi
hái kěyǐ yòng ne! Wǒ kàn kàn...yǒu "Netflix"! "Disney
Plus"! Hái yǒu gè "Hulu". "Hulu" shì shénme? Zhè
zhēnshi tài shénqíle! Yǒu "HBO Max" ma?[21]

PAZ: *(OS)* 别管那些了! 那些驾驶员去哪了? 你先找到他们再
看电视吧。 Biéguǎn nàxiēle! Nàxiē jiàshǐ yuán qù nǎle? Nǐ
xiān zhǎodào tāmen zài kàn diànshì ba.[22]

TUNDE: *(To* COMM*)* 哎呀! 你简直跟我妈一样唠叨。 Āiyā! Nǐ
jiǎnzhí gēn wǒ mā yīyàng lāo dao.[23]

*(*TUNDE *searches the area. He eventually moves a large piece
of debris, uncovering an unconscious* HENRY.*)*

TUNDE: *(To* COMM*)* Paz! 我找到一个驾驶员了! 他还活
着。 Paz! Wǒ zhǎodào yīgè jiàshǐ yuánle! Tā hái huózhe.[24]

18　Still operational. They are still asleep, thank The
Founders.

19　Wow. *My God!* Look at this!

20　What? What is it?

21　Their entertainment system can still be used! Let me
see... there is "Netflix"! "Disney Plus"! There is also "Hulu".
What is "Hulu"? This is amazing! Is there "HBO Max"?

22　Leave that alone! Where did the pilots go? Find them
first before watching TV.

23　Ai ya! You are nagging like my mother.

24　Paz! I found a pilot! He is still alive.

PAZ: *(OS)* 是白人吗? Shì báirén ma?[25]

TUNDE: *(To* COMM*)* 不是, 那是个中国人。我看看他状况怎样。 Bú shì, nà shì gè zhōng guó rén. Wǒ kàn kàn tā zhuàngkuàng zěnyàng.[26]

*(*TUNDE *checks on* HENRY's *vital signs very gently and carefully.* HENRY *starts to revive.)*

HENRY: Who—?

TUNDE: 你好。你说中文吗? Nǐ hǎo. Nǐ shuō zhōngwén ma?[27]

HENRY: I'm sorry. I don't speak Chinese. I'm American.

TUNDE: Ah! English! American English? Outstanding! Hey, you are my first American English speaker! But you're Chinese?

HENRY: Japanese. Well…Japanese-American.

TUNDE: Ooooh! Oh, I understand. But you live in America?

HENRY: I did. Ow!

TUNDE: Oh, are you okay, sir? Let me help you sit. *(In Yoruba) O ya!*[28]

HENRY: Thanks. *(Notices the window)* Sunlight. That—that's sunlight!

TUNDE: Yes.

HENRY: We landed? We're still alive?! Holy moly! *(He looks out the broken window.)* We are on the right side of the sky! Yes! We made it!

---

25 Is it the white man?

26 No, it's a Chinese guy. Let me see how he is.

27 Hello. Do you speak Mandarin?

28 Come on!

TUNDE: It was quite the entrance. My name is Tunde. I am the local security officer in this region. I apologize if my English is not wonderful. I am out of practice.

HENRY: No, your English is great! How did you learn it?

TUNDE: I've always spoken it. Some of my ancestors were from Nigeria. English was actually one of the official languages! The British colonized us!

HENRY: The British will do that.

TUNDE: Unfortunately, I don't have practice speaking English these days. Mr...?

HENRY: Call me Henry.

TUNDE: Henry. Tell me, how many were there like you in America?

HENRY: What do you mean?

TUNDE: Um... Not white? Japanese. How many?

HENRY: Dude. We just crash landed after traveling a bazillion light years from Earth onto an alien planet. And that's the first thing you want to know?

TUNDE: I was curious. We have some old American film and TV here. Like *Friends*...and, and, *Seinfeld*. But I don't know if I see many Japanese people on those shows.

HENRY: Yeah, tell me about it. You have *some* American shows?

TUNDE: Yes. Some were on those first ships. People took them as carry ons. DVDs. Blu-Ray. Ancient formats. A smattering. Much was lost in the Great Abandonment. Here we have mostly a lot of old Chinese films. Mexican Telenovela... A lot of Bollywood, of course, if you like that.

HENRY: "The Great Abandonment" did you say?

TUNDE: Oh wait! You are from Seattle, yes? *Frasier* was from Seattle! "Tossed salad and scrambled eggs!" Right? Right?

HENRY: Uh—

TUNDE: What does that mean? "Tossed salad and scrambled eggs?"

HENRY: I don't actually know. They're foods. I don't know why he's singing about them, though.

TUNDE: Still a mystery, then. I was hoping you'd know. Sorry for all my questions! I never thought I'd meet a living American. I studied you all in university, and now you are here.

HENRY: In university?

TUNDE: Yes. I majored in Classics. I wrote my thesis on Tarantino.

HENRY: "Classics"?

TUNDE: Yes. My parents said I should study something more modern but there are only so many earnest tributes to our founders that you can watch. Like: "And so the people of the six ships forged on despite hardship..." So boring! But life before the Great Abandonment... In my thesis I had to write about how American movies were decadent and indecent. But really I secretly admire them. I always say: The only way to talk about some issues is to examine them in another time. So I'm excited to see what we can learn from this ship. It's like a museum of America crashlanded in my backyard!

HENRY: Right. Look, Not that I'm uninterested in your thesis, but is this ship intact? Did the stasis pods survive the crash?

TUNDE: Yes. My partner is checking on the systems, but it seems okay. When the backup team arrives we'll do a full assessment.

HENRY: Thank God. When I see Emerson I'll have to thank him for the landing. Where is he?

TUNDE: The pilot? We don't know. You are the first we find. Hey, can I ask you something?

HENRY: Sure.

TUNDE: You know that the Japanese didn't treat the Chinese very well in World War II? Right?

HENRY: Yeah, I don't think they did. *(Pause)* Was that a question?

TUNDE: We learned that in school. Slave camps. Turned their women into prostitutes.

HENRY: Oh. Oh! That was well before my time.

TUNDE: Was it?

HENRY: Yeah. Like… Sixty years before I was born. I had nothing to do with oppressing any Chinese people, trust me.

TUNDE: Hmm… But still. We know about things.

HENRY: Hey, so why do you speak Chinese when you aren't… Uh…I mean, you're…not Chinese. Right?

TUNDE: Oh, well. First, I am part Chinese. One quarter. Most everyone is a little bit of everything here in *Yeni Dünya.*

HENRY: Really?

TUNDE: Yes. But mostly because it's the main language here. If you want to work in government, you learn Mandarin.

HENRY: Really?

TUNDE: Yes. One of the founding ships was from Beijing, and they were the ones to set up a… *Oro kan wa fun…*[29] What do you call government systems in

—————
29 There's a word for it…

English? Like permits, regulations, taxes. There's a word...

HENRY: Bureaucracy?

TUNDE: *(In Yoruba) Beeni!*[30] Bureaucracy! When we arrived, the Chinese created all of the bureaucracy here—

HENRY: Oh, of course they did.

TUNDE: And that's why we speak Mandarin. Up at the higher levels, anyway. Chinese is the language of culture and commerce. English, kind of unfashionable. Many don't bother to learn it. Except those with nostalgia, like me!

HENRY: You said one of the ships that made it was from China. How many ships made it here?

TUNDE: Six.

HENRY: Six? Six total?

TUNDE: Yes.

HENRY: We launched, like, seven hundred of them! All these massive ships... And you're telling me only six made it? What happened to all the other ones?

TUNDE: They didn't make it. It was a long ass journey, so many things could go wrong. We were just the lucky ones.

HENRY: Just six.

TUNDE: Yes, and every school child knows each from Grade 1. *(Singsong—a kid's tune learned by rote)* Arclight 7, from Beijing, China, brought governmental organization and efficiency. Arclight 53, from Lagos, Nigeria brought mineral resource expertise. Arclight 93, from Salvador de Bahia, Brazil, brought love of sport and dance. Arclight 146, from Bangalore, India, brought spiritual enlightenment and forward thinking,

---

30   Yes!

Arclight 282, from Mexico City, Mexico, brought
expert cuisine and work ethic. And Arclight 455,
from Istanbul, Turkey, brought heavenly music and
hospitality.*(/Singsong)* And your ship would make 7!
We have to rewrite our schoolbooks.

HENRY: So...China, Brazil... Um...

TUNDE: Nigeria, India, Mexico, and Turkey.

HENRY: So... None from the US?

TUNDE: None from United States. None from European
Union, too. Crazy, right? It's like... 那是什么词 Nà shì
shénme cí...?[31] *Karma!* That's the word. Hey, is it true
what they say about the white Americans?

HENRY: What do they say?

TUNDE: They all had guns. And they shot all the blacks
all the time.

HENRY: No. That.... That's an exaggeration. Kind of.
You guys really don't know...I guess you didn't have a
lot of Americans or Europeans on those first ships?

TUNDE: No. Very few. In the beginning, less than ten
percent. And many were 外国人 Wàiguó rén.[32]

HENRY: I'm sorry, what?

TUNDE: Um... What did Americans call those who
moved away from one country to go to another?

HENRY: "Illegals"? Or... "Expatriates"... if they had
money.

TUNDE: Right, many of the whites were "Expatriates"
from white countries at time of departure. And today?
Almost all people mixed by now. No one just white
here.

HENRY: Is that why you fired tiny spaceships at us?

---

31 What is that word?

32 Foreigners

TUNDE: We all saw. The Committee said you left your orbit, started an invasion. They had to defend *Yeni Dünya*.

HENRY: But, were they ever going to let us land?

TUNDE: The Committee always considers wisely. They consider all options. Eventually I think they would decide to let in the children, let them learn our world and culture. And only then we revive some adults. Maybe just the desireables. You see?

HENRY: I'm beginning to.

TUNDE: Not the white ones! *(Laughs)* But seriously, even if we decide you're okay, we have to make sure you have all the vaccines and can adjust, find you jobs. You believe in the vaccines, right?

HENRY: Uh... Yes. Of course.

TUNDE: Some people proposed drafting a loyalty pledge in order to join us. Or limited guest status with re-education. Um... *(In Yoruba) Kilo tun ku?*[33] Sterilization? Lots of little details. But then your pilot friends took the decision out of our hands.

HENRY: We were damaged. We had to land.

TUNDE: Who told you this?

HENRY: Emerson. The pilot.

TUNDE: Can you trust him to tell the truth? He is one of *them.* 美国人Měiguó rén.[34] American liars. We learned all about ancient Americans in school. The cautionary tales, my goodness!

HENRY: Emerson wasn't lying about this. I'd trust a pilot when he tells me he has to land the ship.

---

33   What else?

34   American.

TUNDE: *Awon...*[35] That's interesting....

(Suddenly, TUNDE's communicator pipes up.)

PAZ: *(OS)* Tunde! 这是Paz! 请回应! Tunde! Zhè shì Paz! Qǐng huí yìng![36]

TUNDE: *(To* COMM*)* Paz, 我听见了。Paz, wǒ tīngjiànle.[37]

PAZ: *(OS)* Tunde, 我找到她了! 我找到那个女的了。Tunde, wǒ zhǎodào tāle! Wǒ zhǎodào nàgè nǚ de le.[38]

(We hear the panicked voice of RUSSELL.*)*

RUSSELL: *(OS)* Please hear me out! We don't mean any harm! We come in peace!

PAZ: *(OS)* 安静! 闭上你的嘴巴! 我们在Yeni不说英文。我们说中文! 中文! Ānjìng! Bì shàng nǐ de zuǐbā! Wǒmen zài Yeni bù shuō yīngwén. Wǒmen shuō zhōngwén! Zhōngwén![39] No English here!

RUSSELL: *(OS)* Aah! Okay, Okay!

TUNDE: *(To* COMM*)* Paz, 让我跟那个女的说话。拜托。Paz, ràng wǒ gēn nàgè nǚ de shuōhuà. Bàituō.[40]

PAZ: *(OS)* 随便你。Suíbiàn nǐ.[41]

TUNDE: *(To* COMM*)* Excuse me. Missus captain. Can you hear me?

RUSSELL: *(OS)* Yes.

TUNDE: *(To* COMM*)* I am Tunde. I am glad you are alive. How are you?

---

35 Interesting

36 Tunde! This is Paz! Please respond!

37 Paz, I hear you.

38 Tunde, I found her. I found the woman.

39 Be quiet! Shut your mouth! We don't speak English in Yeni. We speak Chinese! Chinese!

40 Paz, let me talk to that woman. Please.

41 Whatever you want.

RUSSELL: *(OS)* I'd feel a lot better if there wasn't a gun pointed at my head.

TUNDE: *(To* COMM*)* Paz, 她说你的枪让她很紧张。Paz, tā shuō nǐ de qiāng ràng tā hěn jǐnzhāng.[42]

PAZ: *(OS)* 我就希望她紧张! Wǒ jiù xīwàng tā jǐnzhāng![43]

TUNDE: *(To* COMM*)* Captain, I want to say that you are extremely lucky.

RUSSELL: *(OS)* Why's that?

TUNDE: *(To* COMM*)* You managed to land in a very remote area. Nova Amazônia. We are only ones anywhere close. If you had landed in a populated area, you would be in much trouble.

RUSSELL: *(OS)* Sure. "Lucky".

TUNDE: *(To* COMM*)* Now, I need you to return to the bridge. Your friend Henry is also here. Say "Hello", Henry.

HENRY: *(To* COMM*)* Uh, Hello, Captain.

RUSSELL: *(OS)* Hello Henry.

TUNDE: *(To* COMM*)* Now, will you come peacefully with Paz? Or…will we have to use other methods? You choose.

RUSSELL: *(OS)* Fine. I'll go with her.

TUNDE: *(To* COMM, *in Yoruba) Ese,*[44] Captain! Paz! 请把那个女的带到舰桥上。Paz! Qǐng bǎ nàgè nǚ de dài dào jiàn qiáo shàng.[45]

---

42   Paz, she said your gun makes her nervous.

43   I hope I make her nervous!

44   Thank you

45   Paz! Please take that woman to the bridge.

PAZ: *(OS)* 听到了。*(To* RUSSELL*)* 快点! 动作快点!
Tīng dàole. *(To* RUSSELL*)* Kuài diǎn! Dòngzuò kuài
diǎn![46]

HENRY: You still have guns? Like the ones we had?

TUNDE: *(In Yoruba) Beeni.*[47] Want to see?

*(*TUNDE *casually holds out his gun for* HENRY *to see.*
HENRY *could easily snatch it if he wanted. But he doesn't.*
HENRY *just looks.)*

HENRY: I, uh, thought you'd have lasers or blasters
by now. All this time here and your guns look pretty
much the same.

TUNDE: Yes. We have not improved upon American
way of killing. That is true. *(He casually holsters his gun.)*
Once we find Mr Emerson we can leave. Start to get
you… 那是什么词Nà shì shénme cí...?[48] The word that
means "get you ready to become one of us"?

HENRY: Assimilated?

TUNDE: 对! Duì![49] You will be assimilated!

HENRY: Terrific. Where would we go?

TUNDE: Outside. We set up a holding area.

HENRY: Outside. Outside the ship? I'd set foot onto a…
alien planet?

TUNDE: Not alien planet. To *Yeni Dünya.* That's Turkish
for "New World". Nice, huh? Before we came, it was
an alien planet. Hostile animals, poison atmosphere,
deadly disease.

HENRY: We wondered what it'd be like, here.

---

46   I hear you. Hurry up! Hurry up!

47   Yes.

48   What word is that?

49   Yes!

TUNDE: So harsh! Less than ten percent of settlers who arrived survived the first ten years! Harsh world, harsher people! So much conflict.

HENRY: But not anymore?

TUNDE: The people of the six ships, we had so little in common but we became one people. No other choice. We even pass laws to force us to marry outside of our own race. A few generations, no Brazilians, no Turks, no Nigerians. All *Yeni*.

HENRY: You seriously have laws about who you can marry?

TUNDE: Of course! See both the Indian and Chinese forefathers had—

(We hear people approaching.)

PAZ: *(OS)* 往那走！到那边！Wǎng nà zǒu! Dào nà biān![50]

RUSSELL: *(OS)* Alright, alright! I know my own ship!

TUNDE: Another time.

(RUSSELL enters with her hands up, followed by PAZ who is brandishing a gun. PAZ is a Latinx woman but speaks perfect Mandarin. RUSSELL looks a little worse for wear.)

PAZ: Tunde! 你看我对你多好，我还帮你收垃圾呢。Tunde! Nǐ kàn wǒ duì nǐ duō hǎo, wǒ hái bāng nǐ shōu lā jī ne.[51]

(TUNDE and PAZ laugh. HENRY and RUSSELL look bewildered as they don't understand.)

TUNDE: *(To RUSSELL)* She says you seem to be well.

RUSSELL: *(Icily)* I'm fine, thank you.

HENRY: Captain Russell! I was worried about what happened to you. Where did you go? And where's Emerson?

---

50   Go there! Go through!

51   Tunde! You see how nice I am to you, I also help you clean up trash.

RUSSELL: Not now, Mr Hirano.

TUNDE: That's actually a very good question. Where
is Mr Emerson? We expect to find three of you on the
bridge. Instead we only saw Mr Hirano here. And we
found you— *(To* PAZ*)* 你在哪里找到她的? Nǐ zài nǎlǐ
zhǎodào tā de?[52]

PAZ: 在船的后部。脚手架倒塌时砸到她了, 我在地上找到她
的。真是个笨蛋。Zài chuán de hòu bù. Jiǎoshǒujià dǎotā
shí zá dào tāle, wǒ zài dìshàng zhǎodào tā de. Zhēnshì
gè bèndàn.[53]

TUNDE: Apparently you were found near the back of
the ship. That's not where you steer this thing, is it?

RUSSELL: We...I—wanted to check whether the stasis
pods are still functioning. But then the scaffolding
collapsed beneath us.

TUNDE: Mr Emerson was with you?

RUSSELL: Yes.

TUNDE: *(To* PAZ*)* 还有另一个驾驶员。你去找他, 从我们找到
那个女人的地方开始。Hái yǒu lìng yīgè jiàshǐ yuán. Nǐ qù
zhǎo tā, cóng wǒ men zhǎo dào nà gè nǚ rén de dì fāng
kāi shǐ.[54]

PAZ: 好吧。但是...我们先确定这个没问题吧。我不信任
她。Hǎo ba. Dànshì...wǒmen xiān quèdìng zhège méi
wèntí ba. Wǒ bù xìnrèn tā.[55] *(She points to* RUSSELL.*)*

---

52   Where did you find her?

53   At the back of the ship. The scaffold hit her when it
collapsed, and I found her on the ground. What an idiot.

54   There is still the copilot. Go find him, starting from
where we found the woman.

55   All right. But... let's make sure this is secure. I don't
trust her.

TUNDE: 好主意。Hǎo zhǔyì.[56] *(To* RUSSELL*)* Excuse me, miss.

*(*TUNDE *and* PAZ *move and secure* RUSSELL*'s hands with handcuffs, attached to a fixture.)*

RUSSELL: Hey, what are you— What, really?

TUNDE: Just a precaution. Do not resist.

HENRY: Is this really necessary?

TUNDE: Mr Hirano. She disobeyed a direct order to keep the ship in orbit and made an illegal entry into our planet. We hold her for judgment by The Committee.

RUSSELL: What about him?

TUNDE: Henry? He seems to be a reasonable man. Also, he was not involved in the decision to break our laws, was he? I believe he'll be reasonable.

HENRY: Uh, yeah. Mr Reasonable. That's me.

RUSSELL: Oh, for God's sake.

TUNDE: *(To* PAZ*)* 她没问题了。你可以走了。Tā méi wèntíle. Nǐ kěyǐ zǒule.[57] Suerte, mi amiga.[58]

PAZ: 我跟你说过别跟我讲西班牙文。太刺耳了。Wǒ gēn nǐ shuōguò bié gēn wǒ jiǎng xībānyá wén. Tài cì'ěrle.[59]

*(*PAZ *exits.* TUNDE *chuckles.)*

TUNDE: Paz hates when I try to speak Spanish, but how else do you learn?

RUSSELL: Listen. Sir. We didn't have a choice. If we didn't go in we would have all died. A hundred thousand people. Your drone attack damaged the ship.

---

56 Good idea.

57 She is secure. you can go now.

58 Good luck, my friend.

59 I told you not to speak Spanish to me. It's too harsh.

TUNDE: Then stay in the orbit that we set for you. The Committee would not act against you, then.

RUSSELL: We needed to land.

TUNDE: You did not have permission!

RUSSELL: It was promised to us! It was promised to all of us who made the journey. I know it was a long time ago for you, but because of that compact, the US shared technology critical to the creation of the arclights in the first place, that created the escape path that your ancestors took advantage of. Some of those very minds are on board this ship. We are owed the same safe passage as you enjoyed.

TUNDE: Our Committee may say differently.

RUSSELL: This is unbelievable. If the situation was reversed, we would have let you land.

(TUNDE *laughs.*)

TUNDE: On what basis do you say that? If you got here first and we just showed up? I highly doubt that, captain.

RUSSELL: "Give me your tired, your poor/Your huddled masses yearning to breathe free..." Those were the words written on our Statue of Liberty as it welcomed immigrants to our country. Words of welcoming and comfort.

TUNDE: Those are lovely words. Yes. Very lofty. Tell me. Why did your country stop following words like this?

RUSSELL: Oh come on! We never—

TUNDE: These words were not in effect when you closed the border to Mexico at the end. Right? Or when you put Japanese into camps in the World War?

RUSSELL: What does that have to—

TUNDE: Let me finish! Did the huddled masses include slaves you brought from Africa? The native tribes you stole land from? Afghan refugees? Did your huddled masses law protect them?

HENRY: That wasn't actually a law of ours, Tunde. It was just a poem. Kind of an…aspirational poem.

TUNDE: But my point: You Americans were very selective when it came to immigration. A little picky about who entered your country, yes? We are too. We have our own problems. We don't need yours.

RUSSELL: Why do you think we're all such monsters? The way you say "You Americans"…

HENRY: Addie… The people who actually made it here are from places that…may not hold the best opinion of America.

RUSSELL: What? Like Iraq? …Iran?

HENRY: No.

RUSSELL: Canada?

HENRY: No. Just, trust me on this.

RUSSELL: Okay, fine. Look, we just want to get out of this deathtrap! Isn't there some part of the planet you're not using? There must be some sort of way. We saw your footprint. There are vast amounts of unused land here. Let us go there! We'll fend for ourselves.

TUNDE: O ya! Think! Let's say we do that. Best case scenario for us: you all die. Very sad. But say you survive. You grow, you thrive, you expand. Eventually you'll want more. Eventually you'll see us as your rival. For resources. For land. For everything.

RUSSELL: We'll deal with that then.

TUNDE: No, we deal with it now. Tell me, when has any dark skin people in history ever benefit from meeting the white man?

HENRY: We could sign a treaty.

TUNDE: A treaty? *(He laughs.)*

HENRY: What's so funny?

TUNDE: Should we revive a Native of America and ask them how well a treaty with the white man is honored? Come on!

RUSSELL: We are not them! Not all white people are the same!

TUNDE: But your history is infamous! You chose such monsters to lead you! With your democracy! Like that one with the hair! And the one we threw a shoe at!

RUSSELL: Not us! I didn't vote for them— We lived in a Blue State.

TUNDE: *Kini ilu "Blue State"?*[60] What is a "Blue State"?

HENRY: Oh, boy. See, we had this mechanism called the Electoral College. And if you lived in a state that voted for your candidate, then your whole state would count for that candidate.

TUNDE: *(In Yoruba) Ko ye mi.*[61] What's the point of voting then?

HENRY: No. It just had that effect. Let's just say our national leaders weren't always popular in our particular part of the country.

RUSSELL: Right. So it wasn't our fault.

HENRY: We were pretty…progressive in Seattle.

RUSSELL: Yeah, most of the time I voted third party!

TUNDE: Yes, but how can we tell? You all look the same to us. There have been so many miscreants in your country's history. Madmen. Devils. Do you condemn their evil?

---

60   What is a "Blue State"?

61   I don't understand.

RUSSELL: I'm a captain, not a representative of all Americans. But I know there are plenty of very fine people on this ship.

TUNDE: You say that, but, are there racists on board? Are there thieves? Capitalists? Are there firearm worshipers? Nazis? Did your schoolteachers make it on ship? Artists? Factory workers? Or was it just the powerful? The wealthy? The children of the wealthy?

RUSSELL: I can recognize that our history might have some episodes that seem less than savoury to someone who didn't learn all of it. But the horror stories that you guys are throwing around aren't all we're about. It's like if we judged China just from what happened in Tiananmen Square.

TUNDE: Tiananmen Square? How do you know about that place? What do you think happened in Tiananmen Square?

RUSSELL: The... The protesters, the government massacred them. There was that one guy who stood in front of a tank. It's famous.

TUNDE: I never heard this, and it's our history. Must be some old American propaganda, huh?

RUSSELL: Are you kidding me? What the—

HENRY: Addie.

RUSSELL: They're lying about their own history, Henry!

HENRY: Yeah, well... Empires don't always tell the whole story of how they became empires.

TUNDE: Look, I love American culture. Your TV, movies, music. Very entertaining. But you overrate yourself so much! The Roman Empire lasted fifteen hundred years! The Chinese Dynasty four thousand years! America never even reached three hundred years. And it's arrogance destroyed the whole world in its wake.

RUSSELL: Oh for the—

(HENRY *clears his throat to get* RUSSELL'*s attention. He slowly shakes his head "No".)*

RUSSELL: We just want a chance. To redeem ourselves. That's all. Right, Henry?

HENRY: Yes, exactly. It seems to me that maybe our people, once they're revived, can be evaluated on a case by case basis? We could each make a pitch—

RUSSELL: Wait a minute, when we set out no one said anything about having to pass a citizenship test to a foreign government.

TUNDE: We would not accept your kind without some reassurance. You mentioned your ship's delay. A hundred years, right?

RUSSELL: A hundred sixty-five.

TUNDE: A hundred sixty-five years! That's how far from the past you are to us. Just imagine that during your time on Earth someone from a hundred sixty-five years past came to America. What was that long before your time on Earth? The war...*Gone With the Wind.*

HENRY: The Civil War? North versus South.

TUNDE: *Beeni.*[62] Now, The South was on the side of slavery, yes?

HENRY: That's the generally accepted understanding.

TUNDE: Alright, imagine in the year 2020 some South soldiers— "Confederates", right? They just appear, maybe on a boat. They were asleep for a hundred sixty-five years inside of an iceberg, and now they want to rejoin your America. And by the way, they claim the right to hold slaves again, because they never surrendered.

RUSSELL: This is a grossly unfair—

---

62 Yes.

TUNDE: *Ki ni?*[63] You say racism is in your past? You're all in the past to us. You are history come to life. Old ghosts, old thinking. What do you say when we tell you that we don't have Freedom of Speech--

RUSSELL: You don't? Really?

TUNDE: No! Or right to have guns. And Democracy! Ai ya! We don't elect a leader. We have The Committee.

RUSSELL: Oh, that sounds wonderful.

TUNDE: On *Yeni Dünya* the individual serves the collective. I didn't choose this assignment here in the most remote part of *Yeni!* But of course I go!

RUSSELL: But why? Don't you deserve better?

TUNDE: Who cares about me? No one person is more important than our collective needs. To join us you must accept that and surrender your ancient American thinking. Eager to join us still?

HENRY: It beats being frozen in a tube for eternity. I think if you gave us a chance we'd come to accept it.

TUNDE: And what would we get from allowing you in? Maybe don't ask what we do for you, but say what you do for *Yeni Dünya.*

(A beep is heard on TUNDE's *comm unit.)*

TUNDE: Excuse me. *(Talks into his comm)* Paz! 情况如何? Paz! Qíngkuàng rúhé?[64]

PAZ: *(OS)* 我找遍了整个储藏室, 但这里一个人都没有。你问一下我们的客人他在哪里好不好? Wǒ zhǎo biànle zhěnggè chúcáng shì, dàn zhèlǐ yīgè rén dōu méiyǒu. Nǐ wèn yīxià wǒmen de kèrén tā zài nǎlǐ hǎobù hǎo?[65]

---

63 Is it?

64 Paz! How's it going?

65 I searched the entire storage room, but there was no one here. Would you please ask our guest where he is?

TUNDE: *(To* COMM*)* 储藏室? 不是原生舱那里吗? Chúcáng
shì? Bú shì yuánshēng cāng nàlǐ ma? [66]

PAZ: *(OS)* 不, 我很确定是在储藏室。Bù, wǒ hěn quèdìng
shì zài chúcáng shì. [67]

TUNDE: Paz says she can't find your friend. Where do
you think he might be?

RUSSELL: I don't know. We were making sure the stasis
pods survived.

TUNDE: Paz tells me you were nowhere near the stasis
pods. If it turns out you don't tell the truth—

RUSSELL: I'm telling the truth. I don't know where he is.

TUNDE: *(To* COMM*)* Paz, 这女的说她不知道。Paz, zhè nǚ
de shuō tā bù zhīdào. [68]

PAZ: *(OS)* 好吧, Tunde。我再找找看。Hǎo ba, Tunde. Wǒ
zài zhǎo zhǎo kàn... [69] *¡Ah chingar!* [70]

TUNDE: *(To* COMM*)* 什么? 你看到什么? Shénme? Nǐ kàn
dào shénme? [71]

PAZ: *(OS) Dios mio!* [72] 是另外一个白人! 他还活着。他好苍白
喔, 这是正常的吗? Shì lìngwài yīgè báirén! Tā hái huózhe.
Tā hǎo cāngbái o, zhè shì zhèngcháng de ma? [73]

TUNDE: She says she found your friend.

RUSSELL: How is he?

---

66 Storage room? Weren't they at the stasis pods?

67 No, I'm pretty sure it was the storage room.

68 Paz, the woman said she didn't know.

69 Okay, Tunde. I'll look for him again...

70 Fuck!

71 What? What do you see?

72 By God!

73 It's the other white person! He's still alive. He is so pale,
is this normal?

PAZ: *(OS)* 混蛋, 不要动! Húndàn, búyào dòng!
Wǒ yǒu qiāng![74]

EMERSON: *(OS)* Miss? I need medical assistance. My
name is Morris Emerson. Pilot.

RUSSELL: *(To* COMM*)* Emerson! Are you alright?

TUNDE: *(To* RUSSELL*)* Don't talk!

PAZ: *(OS)* 不准动! 一根汗毛都不准动! Bù zhǔn dòng! Yī
gēn hànmáo dōu bù zhǔn dòng![75]

EMERSON: *(OS)* Lady, my arm is broke. My ankle's
fucked up. I fell two levels. It took me an hour to go up
one flight of stairs. I ain't going nowhere. I surrender,
okay? Just get me to a hospital. See? Ow! Hands up.

RUSSELL: He's in pain. Tell her he's in pain. He needs
medical help!

TUNDE: *(To* COMM*)* Paz! 小心点, 他受伤了! 他很危险! Paz!
Xiǎoxīn diǎn, tā shòushāngle! Tā hěn wēi xiǎn![76]

RUSSELL: *(To* COMM*)* Emerson! Do you hear me?

EMERSON: *(OS)* Yo! Russell! Is that you?

PAZ: *(OS)* 不准动!!! 我最后一次警告你! Bù zhǔn dòng!!!
Wǒ zuìhòu yīcì jǐnggào nǐ![77]

EMERSON: *(OS)* Lady, for the love of—

(Three gunshots are heard. Then nothing)

TUNDE: *(To* COMM*)* Paz! Paz! 我们听到枪声了。请回
报。Paz! Paz! Wǒmen tīng dào qiāng shēngle. Qǐng
huíbào.[78]

74　　Bastard, don't move! I have a gun!

75　　Don't move! Don't move a single hair!

76　　Paz! Be careful, he is injured! He is dangerous!

77　　Don't move!!! I warn you one last time!

78　　Paz! Paz! We heard gunshots. Please report back.

PAZ: *(OS)* 我还好。刚刚实在太危险了。他动作好快。Wǒ
hái hǎo. Gānggāng shízài tài wēi xiǎnle. Tā dòngzuò hǎo
kuài.[79] Por dios.[80]

TUNDE: *(To* COMM*)* 他还活着吗? Tā hái huózhe ma?[81]

PAZ: *(OS)* 我把他射死了。他正要攻击我, 所以我朝他的胸膛
开了三枪。Wǒ bǎ tā shè sǐle. Tā zhèng yào gōng jī wǒ,
suǒyǐ wǒ cháo tā de xiōngtáng kāile sān qiāng.[82]

TUNDE: *(To* COMM*)* 我明白。Wǒ míngbái.[83]

RUSSELL: What... What happened? What is it?

TUNDE: Your friend. He tried to assault Paz. She acted
in self-defense. I'm sorry.

RUSSELL: No! No! You killed him? No!

TUNDE: He should have listened and complied.

RUSSELL: He had a broken arm and leg! That's what he
said! You heard him, right? He couldn't hurt her. She's
lying!

TUNDE: Officer Paz would not lie. Your friend should
have remained compliant. He caused his own death.

RUSSELL: He was a good man.

HENRY: I'm so sorry, Addie. I'm so—

RUSSELL: Fuck off, Henry! Morris didn't deserve this.
We don't deserve this.

HENRY: I know, but... What's done is done. We're in
this together.

---

79   I'm fine. It was very scary here just now. He moves so
fast.

80   By God.

81   Is he still alive?

82   I shot him to death. He was about to attack me, so I shot
him three times in the chest.

83   I understand.

RUSSELL: Are we? Because I seem to be shackled to the wall and you're walking around as you please. Have you noticed that?

(TUNDE's *communicator beeps.*)

PAZ: *(OS)* Tunde!

TUNDE: *(To* COMM*)* 什么? Shénme?[84]

PAZ: *(OS)* 请下来看看这个! Qǐng xiàlái kàn kàn zhège![85]

TUNDE: *(To* COMM*)* 现在吗? Xiànzài ma?[86]

PAZ: *(OS)* 对。我在七号甲板。Duì. Wǒ zài qī hào jiǎbǎn.[87]

TUNDE: *(To* COMM*)* 对. Hai.[88] *(He turns to* HENRY.*)* I have to meet with my partner. Sir. Give me your hand.

(HENRY *does.* TUNDE *slaps on a bracelet.*)

HENRY: What's this?

TUNDE: It just tells us where you are. Do not move from this room until we return! For your own safety. Understand?

(HENRY *nods.*)

TUNDE: I'll be back. *(He exits.)*

HENRY: Great. They chipped me like some housepet.

RUSSELL: They're gone. C'mon, quick. Help me get out of these.

HENRY: What?

RUSSELL: The handcuffs. Get them off me and we can escape. There's a cutting tool in that panel there. They're careless!

---

84   What?

85   Please come down and take a look at this!

86   Now?

87   Yes. I'm on deck seven.

88   Yes.

HENRY: Escape and do what?

RUSSELL: Get help. The stasis pods are still operating. But the landing damaged LANA. We can't release everyone until she reboots, but we can revive people manually if we hurry.

HENRY: But where would we go?

RUSSELL: I've been exploring this ship for two and a half decades. I could play hide and seek here for years. Trust me.

(HENRY *points to his tracking bracelet.*)

HENRY: I have this piece of jewelry now, though.

RUSSELL: So? We just cut it off. There's some scissors in there, too.

HENRY: Let's say we escape. What would we do?

RUSSELL: Revive the others?! Or get the hell out of here, maybe? Run for our lives? You could jump out that window for all I care. Just free me.

HENRY: But they'd find us. They'd kill us. Or nature would. We don't know this planet.

RUSSELL: I'm in handcuffs. They killed Emerson. I'll take my chances with the great unknown. I have training in survival, hand to hand combat, you name it. Just release me!

HENRY: They'll come after us.

RUSSELL: So what? You saw how they brought this ship down. By flinging crap at us! These backwards hicks don't have death rays, just Barney Fife there. We can beat them if we just—

(RUSSELL *notices* HENRY's *not moving*)

RUSSELL: Are you going to help me get out? Avenge Emerson?

(HENRY *does not move.*)

RUSSELL: Goddammit! You think you're one of them.

HENRY: I mean they treat me okay.

RUSSELL: Do you think that's going to last? "First they came for the whiteys, and I did nothing, because I'm not white."

HENRY: Addie—

RUSSELL: Fuck you Hirano! You're a racist, too!

HENRY: I'm not!

RUSSELL: You are! You think we deserve this. Us white people.

HENRY: Most of my friends are white. I lived in Seattle for God's sake.

RUSSELL: Are any of them in the stasis pods? Because if your new buddies have their way, your old friends might be turned into compost before too long. But I have a responsibility for everyone on the ship.

HENRY: I just think we can talk to these guys. Appease them. Buy time. Advocate incrementally. We can show them we mean them no harm—

RUSSELL: Yeah? Like Emerson? Remember him? The reason you're even walking around on this godforsaken planet? They shot him when he was in full surrender. They're not going to give folks like us a fair shake.

HENRY: But when you say "us", who is "us", though?

RUSSELL: Why do you keep saying, "Who is 'us'?" Us. Americans. Land of the Free, Home of the Brave. Remember that?

HENRY: Tunde said after I'm cleared medically I can start the process of assimilation into their culture. If I assimilate then I can help you. And together we can change their view about Americans.

RUSSELL: You can't be serious.

HENRY: Our people are all sleeping in the pods, anyway. What's the difference? If I run they'll never trust anyone on this ship.

RUSSELL: You're one of "us" too. Why would they trust you? You're an American.

HENRY: I am, and I'm not.

RUSSELL: What in the world does that mean?

HENRY: It means there were different levels of being American. You're on one level, I'm on another. My grandpa was a farmer in California. During World War II they put him in an internment camp. They took his farm away, never got it back.

RUSSELL: What does that have to do with anything?

HENRY: I'm just...used to the rules of being in the minority. Don't make waves, don't set yourself apart, except in the ways you're expected to be different. Fit in. Get along. Be harmless. Be blameless. Wait your turn. When it comes down to it, this planet doesn't seem different for me than home. Half a galaxy away, still the model minority. You can learn how to do this.

RUSSELL: Hell no. They want us to be ashamed of what we were. You might be. I'm not. I earned my accomplishments. Never needed a handout or quota. We deserve freedom, at least, the people on this ship who actually deserve to be on the ship.

(HENRY *looks at* RUSSELL. *He has a realization.*)

HENRY: Quota! That's it! Oh my God. "Adelaide Russell." Now I remember where I've heard your name before!

RUSSELL: Do you?

HENRY: We studied your case in Law School. *Russell v. Stanford University.* That was you, right? You're "Addie on the Waitlist"!

RUSSELL: What of it?

HENRY: *Russell v. Stanford:* a wide ranging lawsuit alleging discrimination against whites due to affirmative action. That one decision overturned a lot of programs intended to foster diversity in higher ed.

RUSSELL: The university had a duty to select the best students regardless of race, class, and gender. Why should some…

HENRY: It costs a lot to take a case to the Supreme Court, doesn't it? I remember reading about all the various political groups who backed your case.

RUSSELL: That's in no way relevant—

HENRY: The arclight space pilot program. Pretty competitive, right?

RUSSELL: Very much so.

HENRY: My cousin applied. Class valedictorian, three sport athlete, ROTC, Dean's list… She didn't make the first cut. I guess she's long dead by now. How were your grades?

RUSSELL: Fuck you! I worked so hard to get in! I had to overcome so much, as a woman in the Arclight program?! Fuck you! You're not going to tell me I don't deserve to be here!

HENRY: Everyone deserves to be here, but only… What? One percent of humanity got on board? The other ninety-nine percent were left to their fate on a dying planet. We didn't take the hundred thousand most deserving folks, did we? We took the ones who could get a ticket.

RUSSELL: Are you done? Because, let's not forget I landed us here. Didn't I? Seven hundred goddamn ships sailed to their doom, but Captain Adelaide Russell succeeded. So fuck your judgmental

insinuations. I'm damn good at this. And you owe me
your life.

HENRY: Look…we're not making the rules here. Can
we try to figure out a way that we can fit in-

RUSSELL: Maybe you could. I'm married to a woman.
Did you know that? Do you think your new friends
would allow me to hold my wife's hand in public?
They don't have free speech, how do you think they
are on gay rights?

HENRY: I'm guessing probably not great. They're kind
of… It's like we crashed landed onto Space North
Korea. They had this song and dance about how the
people of the six ships banded together and sang
Kumbaya and survived and became one. But these
weren't the Peace and Love All Stars back home. If
I had to guess, they probably tried to kill each other
on this rock until working together became the only
option.

RUSSELL: And you want me to fit in here?

HENRY: I want you to not get us all killed! I'm trying to
protect you!

RUSSELL: Why? So we can join this nightmare? This
isn't a just society!

HENRY: Neither was ours! There's always someone left
out of every society. But you never—

(A knock on the door)

TUNDE: (OS) Hello! Still here?

RUSSELL: Speak of the Devil.

(TUNDE and PAZ reenter carrying EMERSON.)

TUNDE: I see that you have been making yourself
comfortable. Good.

RUSSELL: Morris! Put him down immediately, you…
you animals!

TUNDE: As you wish.

(*They set down the body.*)

RUSSELL: Let me out of here! I have to—

TUNDE: Uh uh uh! We have other issues at hand, I'm afraid.

HENRY: Can you give her a moment, man?

TUNDE: We have rules we must follow. Security protocols. You understand. Can we proceed?

(*A beat*)

RUSSELL: I will remember this.

TUNDE: First of all, my partner wants you to know that she is very sorry she used deadly force. She was so scared by his sudden appearance she was in a panic.

PAZ: 我还是认为我们该把她也给杀了。简单多了。Wǒ háishì rènwéi wǒmen gāi bǎ tā yě gěi shāle. Jiǎndān duōle.[89]

TUNDE: Paz says that she's very sorry.

RUSSELL: You're sorry? He's dead and you're sorry?

TUNDE: It was interesting where he was. The scaffolding that collapsed, it was by the storage area. Not the section for the stasis pods so much as the armory. Your guns, your weapons. Was that what you were trying to get?

RUSSELL: We have a responsibility for the welfare of—

TUNDE: You have a responsibility to follow our orders! Again and again! How do we trust anyone here when you act like this?

RUSSELL: I was defending the innocent travelers on this ship that are my responsibility! It's my duty to deliver them here, safely.

---

89 I still think we should kill her too. Much simpler.

TUNDE: You have no right to be on this planet until we decide that you do! You did not break the land, you did not sacrifice to pain and hardship to turn this hostile planet into one that accepts human life!

RUSSELL: I have the right to a fair trial. Mr Hirano can be my lawyer.

HENRY: Me?

TUNDE: You have whatever rights we assign to you! The people who survived the near death of the human race, only we have rights as citizens of *Yeni*. We are citizens, you are illegal aliens until we say otherwise. Understand? *(Pause)* Ah. My friends. This is such a momentous occasion. The arrival of a new ship long after we believed all was lost. I just wish it was not marred by the violence that this man caused. *(He indicates* EMERSON's *body.)*

RUSSELL: How dare you—

HENRY: Hey hey hey, Captain, this isn't going to do any good—

RUSSELL: But he just—

HENRY: I know. It never does any good. Remember.

RUSSELL: You're just supposed to take this?

HENRY: Yes. It sucks. But yeah. I know, he was a good man. But for his sake we have to survive this. For the greater good.

TUNDE: *Wo?*[90] This one gets it! We'll take you out after for beer! And maybe "hamburgers" in "Americatown"!

HENRY: I think we could all use a drink, right now. Or even another cup of coffee.

TUNDE: Coffee? You drink Coffee?

HENRY: Yeah.

---

90 Do you see?

TUNDE: On this ship? There is coffee?

HENRY: Yeah. Starbucks. It's the first thing I had when—

TUNDE: Starbucks! Thank the founders! Starbucks coffee! 哇! Wa![91]

PAZ: 那是什么? 你为什么这么开心? Nà shì shénme? Nǐ wèishéme zhème kāixīn?[92]

TUNDE: 咖啡! 船上有咖啡! Kāfēi! Chuánshàng yǒu kāfēi![93]

PAZ: 真的吗? 真的咖啡?不是那些恶心的仿冒品? Zhēn de ma? Zhēn de kāfēi? Bú shì nàxiē ěxīn de fǎngmào pǐn?[94]

TUNDE: 他们不就这么说了吗? 星巴克。Tāmen bù jiù zhème shuōle ma? "Starbucks".[95]

PAZ: 啊! 星巴克。A! "Xīngbākè." [96]

HENRY: You don't have coffee here?

TUNDE: No! We weren't able to grow it. We've only heard the stories. And Starbucks! Oh, you must take me to it. Paz can watch the captain.

HENRY: I only know my pod. Unless the captain—

RUSSELL: Buzz off. I'm not telling you anything.

TUNDE: We'll find it without her help. These whites can be so problematic. Just like we've heard. *O ya!*[97] *(To* PAZ*)* Paz! 没什么好担心的,对吧? 我带这个假中国

---

91   Wow!

92   What is that? Why are you so happy?

93   Coffee! There's coffee on board here!

94   Really? Real coffee? Not those disgusting fakes?

95   That's what they just said. "Starbucks".

96   Ah! "Starbucks".

97   Come!

人去找咖啡。Paz! Méishénme hǎo dānxīn de, duì ba? Wǒ dài zhè gè jiǎ zhōng guó rén qù zhǎo kā fēi.[98]

PAZ: 好。也给我带一点吧。Hǎo. Yě gěi wǒ dài yīdiǎn ba.[99]

(TUNDE *and* HENRY *leave,* PAZ *looks over to* RUSSELL. *A long silence.* PAZ *casually approaches* RUSSELL.)

RUSSELL: Hi. Um…I was wondering—

(PAZ *violently clubs* RUSSELL *with her fist.*)

RUSSELL: Ow!

PAZ: 你这愚蠢的贱货。你们摧毁了自己的星球后还敢来我们的? 真不要脸。Nǐ zhè yúchǔn de jiànhuò. Nǐmen cuīhuǐle zìjǐ de xīngqiú hòu hái gǎn lái wǒmen de? Zhēn bú yào liǎn.[100]

(PAZ *strikes* RUSSELL *again.*)

RUSSELL: Uh! Stop! Please!

(*Let's remember that* RUSSELL *is tied in a defenseless position.*)

PAZ: 你这畜生! 上等人在跟你讲话的时候还不闭嘴? Nǐ zhè chùshēng! Shàng děng rén zài gēn nǐ jiǎng huà de shí hòu hái bù bì zuǐ?[101]

(PAZ *slaps* RUSSELL.)

RUSSELL: Um… Hola! Paz? Hola!

---

98 Paz! There is nothing to worry about, right? I will take this sort-of-Chinese guy to find coffee.

99 Good. Bring me some too.

100 You stupid bitch. Do you dare to come to us after destroying your planet? Really shameless.

101 You bastard! You don't know to shut up when your superior is talking to you?

PAZ: 喔, 所以你知道我的名字? 我应该感到感动吗? 你这蠢猴子! Ō, suǒyǐ nǐ zhīdào wǒ de míngzì? Wǒ yīnggāi gǎndào gǎndòng ma? Nǐ zhè chǔn hóuzi![102]

RUSSELL: ¿Hablas Español, si? ¿Hablas Español?[103]

PAZ: *(Surprised)* Yo hablo Español.[104]

RUSSELL: ¡Si! Yo también. Aprender yo español no mucho en la escuela. Un poquito.[105]

(RUSSELL's "Spanish" is slow and halting, but good enough. PAZ calms down a bit.)

PAZ: Yo no sabía que los gringos hablaban algo más que inglés. Suenas horrible. Pero por lo menos el español tuyo suena mejor que el de Tunde.[106]

RUSSELL: Es…difícil saber tu palabras cuando habla muy rápido.[107]

PAZ: ¡OK…hablaré…lento…para…ti…! ¿OK?[108]

RUSSELL: ¡Por favor no…um… "punch" …yo! Yo no problema para tu.[109]

---

102 Oh, so you know my name? Should I be impressed? You stupid monkey!

103 You speak Spanish, right? Do you speak Spanish?

104 I speak Spanish.

105 Yes! Me too. I learn to speak of Spanish in school. A little.

106 I didn't know Americans spoke anything but English. You sound terrible. But your Spanish is better than Tunde, at least.

107 It's… hard to know your words when you speak rapidly.

108 OK… I'll…speak…slow…for…you…! OK?

109 Please no…um… "punch" me! I am no trouble for you.

PAZ: Tú viniste a este planeta. Con eso, sobra de problemas. Pinche idiotas que destruyen todo lo que tocan. Como ratas. O parásitos.[110]

(RUSSELL *doesn't understand fully.*)

RUSSELL: Oh my goodness! ¿Decir algo de "ratas"?[111]

PAZ: 哎呀! 这些该死的外国人! Āiyā! Zhèxiē gāisǐ de wàiguó rén![112]

RUSSELL: Lo siento. No saber por qué pero lo siento. No quiero problema para tu. Lo siento. Yo deseo volar y ir ahora.[113]

PAZ: Ah, si. Pues, lo pudiste haber pensado antes de invadir nuestro planeta.[114]

RUSSELL: "Invadir"? We aren't "invaders". ¿Cómo se dice "refugee"?[115]

PAZ: "Criminal."[116]

(RUSSELL *starts to cry.* PAZ *begins to thaw. Gives her a handkerchief.* RUSSELL *can't reach her own face as she's handcuffed, so* PAZ *dries* RUSSELL's *tears.*)

---

110 You come to this planet. That's trouble enough. You fucking morons destroy everything you touch. Like rats. Or parasites.

111 You said something about "rats"?

112 Ai Ya! These damn foreigners!

113 I'm sorry. I don't know why but I'm sorry. Very sorry. I don't want to cause trouble for you. I'm sorry. I wish I could just fly this and leave now.

114 Yes, well. You should have thought of that before you invaded our planet.

115 "Invader"? We aren't "invaders" How do you say "refugee"?

116 "Criminal"

RUSSELL: Gracias. *(Pause)* ¿Um…es posible ayudar? ¿Por favor?[117]

PAZ: ¿Que onda?[118]

(RUSSELL *motions to* EMERSON'*s body.*)

RUSSELL: Eso hombre. Emerson. Necesitar ir a Señor Emerson.[119]

PAZ: ¿Por qué? Él está muerto. Perdón. No fue mi culpa. El salió de momento y me asustó, yo nada más-[120]

RUSSELL: Necesitar decir mi adiós a Señor Emerson. No saber el futuro. No saber nada. Solo saber dolor en mi corazón.[121]

PAZ: ¿Que? ¿Por eso hombre?[122]

RUSSELL: Eso hombre es todo mi mundo. Yo conducir este— "spaceship"?[123]

PAZ: "Astronave".[124]

---

117 Thank you. Um… Is it possible for a help? Please?

118 What's up?

119 That man. Emerson. I need to go to Mr Emerson.

120 Why? He's dead. I'm sorry. It wasn't my fault. He came out of nowhere and he was very scary, I just—

121 I need to say my goodbye of Mr Emerson. I don't know the future. I don't know anything. All I know is that I have pain in my heart.

122 What? For that guy?

123 That man is all of my world. I drive this… "spaceship?"

124 Spaceship

RUSSELL: Yo conducir este "astronave" con Emerson, solo en cielo, muchos años. Yo quiero tocar él uno más tiempo. Dar beso en la cara.[125]

PAZ: ¿Era tu marido?[126]

RUSSELL: "Married"? No. No es posible. Pero él mi muy, muy amor. Lo siento. Mi Español no es muy bueno por hablar que es decir mi corazón. Por favor. Necesitar decir adiós.[127]

PAZ: ¿Sin problemas? ¿Me lo prometes?[128]

RUSSELL: Sí. De mujer a mujer.[129] I promise, no trouble.

(PAZ *holsters her weapon. She carefully approaches* RUSSELL *and undoes her restraints.* PAZ *keeps her distance and her hand on her weapon.* RUSSELL *slowly gets up.*)

RUSSELL: Gracias.[130]

(RUSSELL *cradles* EMERSON's *body.*)

RUSSELL: Hey there, buddy. It's me. You made it, you amazing pilot, you. Any landing you can walk away from, right? When we get through the other side of this, it'll be my life's mission that your name is never forgotten. Your heroic deeds will live on, Pilot Morris Emerson. Savior of the American people.

---

125 I drive this spaceship with Emerson, alone in the sky, for many years. I want to touch him one more time. Give him a kiss on the face.

126 He was your husband?

127 "Married"? No. It was not possible to marry. But he is my very, very love. I'm sorry. My Spanish is not good enough to talk what is in my heart. Please. I just need to talk goodbye.

128 No problems? You promise?

129 Yes. From one woman to another woman.

130 Thank you.

PAZ: Es como un "Romcom". ¿Sus peliculas romanticas?[131] *(She gestures towards the entertainment system.)*

RUSSELL: Do you even know love, Paz? ¿Conoces el amor?[132]

PAZ: No exactamente. Aquí cuando es tiempo de procrear vamos a una agencia de emparejamiento.¡Así de simple![133]

RUSSELL: Este hombre es más por mi. Amor es más bueno cuando es posible escoger. Paz, tu "society" no es correcto.[134]

PAZ: Tu no sabes ni madre de nuestra sociedad. [135]

RUSSELL: ¿Que tu saber de nuestra sociedad?[136]

PAZ: Tenemos las historias.[137]

RUSSELL: La gente en este astronave es inocente.[138]

TUNDE: *(OS)* Paz! 真的咖啡耶! 太好喝了! Paz! Zhēn de kāfēi ye! Tài hǎo hēle![139]

PAZ: "Inocente". Ningún Americano es inocente.[140]

(HENRY and TUNDE enter. TUNDE holds coffee.)

131 It's like your "Romcom". Your romantic movies?

132 Do you understand love?

133 Not exactly. Here when it's time to mate we go to the matchmaking bureau. Simple!

134 This man is more for me. Love is better when it is possible to choose. Paz, your society is not correct.

135 You don't know anything about our society.

136 Well, what do you know about our society?

137 We have stories.

138 The people on the ship are innocent.

139 Paz! Real coffee! It's so good.

140 "Innocent". No American is innocent.

TUNDE: (*He makes a show of sipping coffee.*) 真的好好喝！
这咖啡的滋味真是苦到我的心坎里去了。我不知道该怎么说
明白。从现在开始, 我— Zhēn de hǎohǎo hē! Zhè kāfēi de
zīwèi zhēnshi kǔ dào wǒ de xīnkǎn lǐ qùle. Wǒ bù zhīdào
gāi zěnme shuō míngbái. Cóng xiànzài kāishǐ, wǒ—[141]
(*He sees that* RUSSELL *is loose.*)

TUNDE: 她在这里做什么? Tā zài zhèlǐ zuò shénme?[142]

PAZ: 没关系的。她只是— Méiguānxi de. Tā zhǐshì—[143]

(RUSSELL, *seeing* PAZ's *attention turned to* TUNDE, *springs
into action. She grabs* PAZ' *weapon.* RUSSELL *takes* PAZ *into
a chokehold from behind, with the gun pointed at her head.*
TUNDE *pulls out his gun in response.*)

TUNDE: Paz! 小心! 小心点! Paz! Xiǎoxīn! Xiǎoxīn diǎn![144]

PAZ: ¡No![145]

RUSSELL: ¡Si, si! ¡Yo soy el jefe! ¿Tu es mala con tu
prisioneros, si? ¡Así que tu mirar a mi ser mala persona
también![146]

TUNDE: Listen, you should know—

RUSSELL: No, you listen to me! Unless you want your
partner's brains splattered all over the wall, it's your
turn to listen to me. Okay?

(*All four characters on pages 82 & 83 simultaneously:*)

---

141 It's incredible! The taste of this coffee is really bitter to
my heart. I don't know how to understand it. From now on,
I—

142 What is she doing here?

143 It's okay. She just—

144 Paz! Be careful! Be careful!

145 No!

146 Yes, yes! I am the boss! You are bad to your prisoners,
yes? Then, you will see me be bad person, too!

RUSSELL:

Yes, I can! Done with the
turn the other cheek shit,
Henry. Not my style.
Time for the Malcolm X
tactics!

That's it, bitch. You tell
him who's in charge now.
Decir a él yo soy jefa
ahora, ¿si?[147]

You put your gun down,
big boy. Then we're all
going to go on a little
walk.
To hell with your society!
It's a communist fascist
Nazi cult.

Today I'm founding New
America. And this is its
capitol, Emersonia! And
you are the ones who
don't belong. Get out of
my country!

HENRY:
Addie! You can' just take a
hostage. It's—

I'm not sure you know
what that means.
Tunde! Do something,
man!

Under control?!

C'mon Addie.
Don't do this.
There has to be another
way.

Can we all get along?

_____

147 Say to him I am the boss, yes?

TUNDE: PAZ:

Paz。你刚刚真的该小心点   Tunde, 对不起啊。
Paz. Nǐ gānggāng   Tunde, duìbùqǐ a.
zhēn de gāi xiǎoxīn diǎn.[148] ("Tunde, sorry.")

我得向管理委员会报告这
个事故! Wǒ dé xiàng   我知道。我不该相信她的。
wěiyuánhuì bàogào   Wǒ zhīdào. Wǒ bù gāi
zhège shìgù![149]   xiāngxìn tā de.[150]
Relax! This is under   ¡Ow! ¡Loca!
control.   ("Ow! You crazy person!")
Miss, this is not the way   他们跟我们想象的一样糟。
to show us you belong in   Tāmen gēn wǒmen
our society.   xiǎngxiàng de yīyàng

但是很好玩耶!   zāo.[151]
美国人来到我们的世界,   Tunde,
十分钟以内我们拿枪对峙!   你停停吧。我很不舒服呢。
Dànshì hěn hǎowán ye!   Tunde, nǐ tíng tíng ba.
Měiguó rén lái dào   Wǒ hěn bù shūfú ne.
wǒmen de shìjiè, shí   ("Tunde, stop this. I am
fēnzhōng yǐnèi wǒmen   very uncomfortable.)
ná qiāng duìzhì![152]   Tunde, 拜托一下!
我没用过这玩意呢!   Tunde, bàituō yīxià!
Wǒ méi yòngguò zhè   ("Tunde, please!")
wányì ne![153]

---

148 Paz. You should really be careful just now.

149 I have to report this incident to the management
committee!

150 I know. I shouldn't have believed her.

151 They are as bad as we thought.

152 This is fun! The Americans come to our world, and
within ten minutes we are facing off with guns!

153 I've never even used this thing!

(TUNDE *laughs, catching everyone's attention.*)

TUNDE: I'm sorry I broke character. This is just so much fun! 我觉得我好像在演一部Tarantino的电影! Wǒ juédé wǒ hǎoxiàng zài yǎn yī bù Tarantino de diànyǐng![154]

(PAZ *laughs too.*)

RUSSELL: ¿Que? ¿Que es gracioso con un pistola en la cabeza?[155]

(TUNDE *lowers his gun and holsters it.*)

TUNDE: Ah, Ms Russell! Pull the trigger. *O ya.*[156] Pull the trigger. Point anywhere.

(RUSSELL *points the gun off to the side. She pulls the trigger. Nothing happens. She tries again. Nothing.* TUNDE *laughs.* PAZ *frees herself from* RUSSELL'*s grip. Grabs her gun*)

PAZ: Dame eso, pinche idiota.[157] *(To* TUNDE*)* 这些人都是笨蛋。你也是! Zhèxiē rén dōu shì bèndàn. Nǐ yěshì![158]

RUSSELL: You don't have real guns? But she shot Emerson—

TUNDE: Her gun is real. But it's configured only for her fingerprint. It will only work for her. For safety.

RUSSELL: You have science fiction guns now?

HENRY: Jesus fucking Christ, Addie! We had these! On Earth! Smart Guns. After the school shooting— Well, one of the school shootings! These aren't new!

RUSSELL: They aren't? Lord forgive me. I've doomed everyone here.

---

154 I feel like I am acting in a Tarantino movie!

155 What? What's so funny with a gun pointed at your head?

156 Go ahead

157 Give me that, fucking idiot.

158 These people are idiots. The same as you!

TUNDE: Even if the gun worked, it would do you no good. The Committee won't talk with terrorists. You kill us or hold us hostage and The Committee will bomb this ship into pieces.

HENRY: They don't care about you?

TUNDE: We are two against lives of all. Easy decision. We are not important.

RUSSELL: My God. It's a whole planet of psychopaths!

TUNDE: See, that is a very American way of—

RUSSELL: Shut up! Shut up! Shut up! I don't want to hear another goddamn ignorant proclamation about what America was or wasn't. You weren't there. We weren't perfect but we would give a damn that one of our soldiers was being held hostage. Do you care that the government is alright with sacrificing your life like that?

TUNDE: "No one person is more important than the collective." That's our motto. Like your Statue of Liberty poem. If government instructs us to do something, we obey. And so, Ms Russell, if you want to live in our society, you—

RUSSELL: No.

TUNDE: —let me finish. Surrender, return to stasis, where you—

RUSSELL: No.

HENRY: Addie, come on. Hear him out.

RUSSELL: No. It's not good enough. I can't allow myself to agree to their terms. I'm—I'm the last American. I'm not going to agree to live in a totalitarian state just for my own survival. There's no way, there's… (*She looks at the dead computer system.*) Yes… There's always a way… (*She moves to a tool panel. pulls out a screwdriver and brandishes it at* PAZ.)

HENRY: Addie! What are- Put down the screwdriver! Don't!

RUSSELL: ¡Paz! ¡Ven aquí![159]

(PAZ *pulls out her gun.* RUSSELL *moves to* PAZ *and acts increasingly threateningly.*)

PAZ: No me obligues a usarlo.[160]

RUSSELL: "Ningún Americano es inocente". ¿Verdad, Paz? "Ningún Americano es inocente".[161]

HENRY: What's happening?

TUNDE: I don't know. Captain Russell, we don't have time for another—

RUSSELL: ¡Me llamo Addie Russell! ¡Soy Americano![162] (*She begins to swing the screwdriver at* PAZ *first and then* TUNDE *threateningly.*) "¡Dame! ¡Dame sus cansadas, sus pobres, sus…muchas personas que quiero mucho más liber—!"[163]

(PAZ *shoots* RUSSELL *several times.* RUSSELL *falls. Silence.* PAZ *takes a breath. She picks up her communicator and calls in a report.*)

PAZ: (*To* COMM) 指挥中心! 这是 Paz。麻烦你告诉管理委员会，这里另一个白人驾驶员拒捕，所以我把她杀了。威胁解除了。Zhǐhuī zhōngxīn! Zhè shì Paz. Máfan nǐ gàosù wěiyuánhuì, zhèlǐ lìng yīgè báirén jiàshǐ yuán jùbǔ, suǒyǐ

159 Paz! Come here!

160 Don't make me use this!

161 "No American is innocent". Right, Paz? "No American is innocent."

162 My name is Addie Russell! I am American!

163 Give me! Give me your tired, your poor! Your… many people who want much more liber-

wǒ bǎ tā shāle. Wēixié jiěchúle.[164] *(She listens, nods. To* COMM*)* 谢谢。我们会在外面等着。Xièxiè. Wǒmen huì zài wàimiàn děngzhe.[165] *(She puts away her communicator.)*

TUNDE: 你为什么射她？又没有必要杀了她。你大可朝她的腿开枪。Nǐ wèishéme shè tā? Yòu méiyǒu bìyào shāle tā. Nǐ dà kě cháo tā de tuǐ kāi qiāng.[166]

PAZ: 有差吗？这些新来者的确有可能被同化，但那个女的是绝对不可能吸收我们的文化的。你也看到她的表现了。有些人就是需要被管教。Yǒu chā ma? Zhèxiē xīn lái zhě díquè yǒu kěnéng bèi tónghuà, dàn nàgè nǚ de shì juéduì bù kěnéng xīshōu wǒmen de wénhuà de. Nǐ yě kàn dào tā de biǎoxiànle. Yǒuxiē rén jiùshì xūyào bèi guǎnjiào.[167]

(PAZ and TUNDE both look to HENRY.)

HENRY: Um, I'm happy to comply with any order or request you might make, guys. Not here to cause any more trouble.

(PAZ and TUNDE exchange a look.)

PAZ: 他们要我们跟疏散小组会面，开始清点资产。我去外面等。Tāmen yào wǒmen gēn shūsàn xiǎozǔ huìmiàn, kāishǐ qīngdiǎn zīchǎn. Wǒ qù wàimiàn děng.[168] Mr Henry.

---

164 Control! This is Paz. Please tell The Committee that the other white pilot here resisted arrest, so I killed her. The threat is over.

165 Thank you. We will wait outside.

166 Why did you shoot her? There is no need to kill her. You could shoot her in the leg.

167 Is there a difference? Some of these newcomers may indeed be assimilated, but it is absolutely impossible for that woman to absorb our culture. You have also seen her behavior. Some people just need to be disciplined.

168 They asked us to meet with the evacuation team and start counting assets. I will wait outside.

(PAZ *offers her hand to* HENRY *to shake. He reluctantly shakes it for an awkward handshake.* PAZ *smiles and exits.* HENRY *takes a moment to survey the carnage, then kneels by the bodies of* EMERSON *and* RUSSELL.)

HENRY: Holy shit, guys. I'm sorry. You both deserved better. You got us all home.

(TUNDE *pats* HENRY's *shoulder.*)

TUNDE: That was rough, my friend. That was rough. Ai ya! I can't believe the amount of paperwork I'll have to do for this one.

HENRY: Yeah. Paperwork.

TUNDE: You don't get ideas, okay?

HENRY: No. No ideas. Not me. *(Pause)* These guys weren't bad people. They were just used to getting their way all the time.

TUNDE: Do you mean these two? Or everyone on the ship?

HENRY: Well, both, probably. But I swear, there are some people in here that… That would fit in here. That could adjust.

TUNDE: We would need proof, Henry. Their track record? We would need proof. *(Pause)* Come, let's go outside then.

HENRY: My God. Outside. Okay. We really made it. *(Looks to the fallen pilots)* Thanks, guys.

TUNDE: Yes. I wish your friends had your outlook.

HENRY: I think they were cooped up in here for too long. Just only talking to themselves.

TUNDE: It's funny. When we heard this ship was from Washington, everyone thought it was Washington the capitol. The DC? They wanted to take out the ship straightaway. At all costs. But of course then we wouldn't have the entertainment system intact. Hey, what you think?

HENRY: About what?

TUNDE: The entertainment! What should we watch first? There was so much culture lost in the journey. So much to discover. I'm very excited to learn. *(He scrolls through selections on screen.)* Joss Whedon! Tyler Perry! Lin Manuel Miranda! Shonda Rhimes! All these treasures that we thought were lost forever. It's so exciting! Where do we even start?

HENRY: There's so much there. You can't go wrong. Do you know about *The Simpsons?* It was a cartoon. Yellow people. Not…like the slur about Asians. Actually colored yellow. It was around forever and it got really bad. But the first…six seasons were magic. You can see what they thought about themselves.[169]

TUNDE: Oh! I can't wait! Come on, let us go.

(TUNDE and HENRY start to exit. TUNDE pauses.)

TUNDE: Hey. "I believe this begins a beautiful friendship!" Good, huh?

HENRY: Close! You were very close! Deep cut!

(TUNDE and HENRY exit. The pilots' bodies are left alone. As lights fade, we see a red light flash. The control system slowly comes back to life.)

COMPUTER VOICE: *(VO)* Reboot complete. Attention! The vital signs of crew members designated in control have been terminated! In order to ensure a

---

169 The producing company can replace this speech with a different sincere pop culture recommendation every performance, so long as it's in character for Henry. Any It Show or movies of today or yesterday. *Sopranos, The Wire, Game of Thrones, Star Wars,* Marvel, whatever. Most every answer will be equally inadequate to the task of explaining all of American culture.

safe arrival, the failsafe system will be reviving the next in line to assume command. Attention!...

(More systems come back online. In the background, a different set of computer voices are heard. The same voice that HENRY *heard during his revival.)*

VOICE: *(VO)* Good morning! We have some good news for you today! To continue in English, select "1"! Para Español, selecc— *Beep* Good morning and welcome back! The ship has now arrived at our destination! Analysis shows the previous crew members designated in control have become incapacitated. As the incoming crew, please take a moment to....

END OF PLAY